Cleveland
Indians
Legends

Cleveland Indians Legends

Russell Schneider

Illustrated by Tom Denny

Black Squirrel Books™

an imprint of The Kent State University Press

Kent, Ohio 44242   www.KentStateUniversityPress.com

Text copyright © 2013 by Russell J. Schneider
Illustrations copyright © 2013 by Tom Denny
Foreword copyright © 2013 by The Kent State University Press, Kent, Ohio
Library of Congress Catalog Number 2012048732
ISBN 978-1-60635-178-9
Manufactured in China

BLACK SQUIRREL BOOKS™ 🐿™
Frisky, industrious black squirrels are a familiar sight on the Kent State
University campus and the inspiration for Black Squirrel Books™, a trade
imprint of The Kent State University Press.
www.KentStateUniversityPress.com

Library of Congress Cataloging-in-Publication Data
Schneider, Russell J.
Cleveland Indians legends / Russell J. Schneider ; illustrated by Tom Denny.
    page   cm
ISBN 978-1-60635-178-9 (hardcover) ∞
1. Cleveland Indians (Baseball team)—History. I. Title.
GV875.C7S345 2013
796.357'640977132—dc23
                                    2012048732

17 16 15 14 13   5 4 3 2 1

To my wife Catherine, for her understanding and
encouragement, and to the many fans of the Indians whose
hopes persevere (though their patience, like mine, is waning).
—*Russ Schneider*

To my children, Lorrain, James, and Sean; and
my grandchildren; to my brothers;
and to my framer and my mentor,
Master Artist William Marsalko
—*Tom Denny*

Contents

Foreword

I am part of the generation of Indians fans who owe their passion and enthusiasm for baseball—Indians baseball specifically—to Russ Schneider. I would wake every morning from February through September, from spring training through the six-month journey that is the beauty of baseball, and rush to read *Batting Around,* the daily notes column authored by Russ in the (Cleveland) *Plain Dealer.*

In my house on Narragansett Drive in Lakewood, the choice was to hustle and get to the paper first, or wait until my father and two older brothers had digested every word. A spirited debate on Indians baseball would follow, all thanks to Russ's unique style of sharing the news and notes of the men in uniform.

Russ began covering the Indians in 1964 (I was nine), and he did so daily until 1977, the year I graduated from Ohio Wesleyan University. Two years later I would have the privilege of working alongside Russ and the other talented baseball writers in the Indians Press Box as a rookie in the Tribe's PR Office.

Russ is, simply, authentic. He loves baseball, especially Indians baseball. And he knows baseball. The one-time minor league catcher becomes beat writer and then, appropriately, one of the top historians on Indians baseball.

So when he decides to write a book about the top players in Indians history, it captures our attention. His was no easy task. More than 1,700 players have worn Indians uniforms since 1901 when the Cleveland franchise was one of the eight charter members of the new American League. Five remain: Detroit, Boston, Chicago, Cleveland, and the Philadelphia Athletics (now the Oakland Athletics).

Smartly, Russ chose to break down the rich 112-year American League history of professional baseball in Cleveland into four eras: 1901–25, 1926–50, 1951–75, and 1976–Present. This is a book about the best of the best, the members of an exclusive group, Tribe legends. Only 10 men per era, 40 top players in all.

Each member is treated to a two-page spread with highlights and an illustration. This is truly the Who's Who of Indians baseball in Russ's eyes and includes some of the greatest names in baseball history.

As is the case with all exclusive clubs or lists, however, there are those who will take issue with who made the cut. Thus, an essential feature of *Cleveland Indians Legends* is Russ's ability to stir debate, a skill honed by his decades as a reporter.

How could he leave off nine-time .300 hitter Charley Jamieson as a member of the Top 10 during the period 1901–25; or AL Batting Champ Bobby Avila in the 1951–75 era; or Joe Carter, the first 30 homer–30 steals guy in Tribe history, as one of the 10 best from 1976 to the present. It's an exercise you will enjoy as you read this wonderful walk through Indians history from Cleveland's quintessential baseball historian.

Bob

DiBiasio

Introduction

Before you ask, here's why we have not included Gaylord Perry and several others among those we consider true "legends" of the Indians. No offense intended and certainly no lack of respect. They simply did not meet a primary criterion we established for membership among the best players of each of their eras (1901–25, 1926–50, 1951–75, and 1976–present).

Unfortunately, Perry wore a Tribe uniform for only 3½ seasons, from 1972 when he was acquired from the San Francisco Giants in one of the best trades Phil Seghi ever made, until—also unfortunately—he was dealt to the Texas Rangers on June 15, 1975.

In those three-plus seasons, Perry won 70 games and lost 57 for Cleveland teams (none of which finished above .500 in those years). During his tenure with the Tribe, Perry won the American League Cy Young award in 1972, when he also was elected the Indians "Man of the Year." It was during the 1974 season that Perry won 15 consecutive games before losing while pitching with an injury that was diagnosed as a severely sprained ankle (after which he never missed a start). Those 15 consecutive victories tied an Indians record set by Johnny Allen in 1937. Perry went on to compile a 314–265 career won-lost record for eight teams over 22 seasons. He was elected to the National Baseball Hall of Fame in 1991 and the Indians Hall of Fame in 2012.

So how can he be left out of this book? Only because—again, unfortunately—his career with the Indians was too brief. Others fall into the same category: Joe Carter, Dennis Eckersley, Len Barker, Roberto Alomar, Bobby Avila, Joe Gordon, Satchel Paige, and even the great Cy Young.

Those who are included are herewith recognized for their outstanding abilities and deeds—and *longevity*—as legends of the Indians by one lifetime fan who has reveled in their successes and lamented their failings, while awaiting another World Series championship.

1901–1925

Addie Joss

He burst into stardom too early—a century too early—but if his deeds had been accomplished in the present era there is little doubt that Adrian "Addie" Joss would be considered one of the premier pitchers in baseball history.

Obviously, none of Joss's contemporaries are alive to verify the brilliance of his tragically all-too-brief career that began in Cleveland in 1902, when the Indians were nicknamed the "Blues." The franchise became the "Indians" in 1914, four years after Joss's untimely demise on April 14, 1911 (two days after his 31st birthday). The cause of his death was reported as an "attack of tubercular meningitis."

A six-foot-three, 185-pound right-hander, Joss had what batters called an "exceptional" curve and an "overwhelming" fastball. Many of them often complained that his pitches seemed to "come out of his hip pocket."

Joss won 160 games and lost 97, with an earned run average of 1.89. Included were at least 20 victories in each of four consecutive seasons (1905–8), 45 shutouts, an equally remarkable 234 complete games (in 268 starts), and 2,327 innings pitched. Equally impressive is that Joss hurled two no-hitters, the first a perfect game on October 2, 1908, against the Chicago White Sox, a game the Indians won, 1–0. The losing pitcher was Ed Walsh, who allowed only four hits. Sportswriters of that era called it "the most stupendous pitching duel of all time."

Two years later, in 1910, prior to the onset of the illness that forced his retirement before the season was more than two months old, Joss pitched another no-hitter, also against the White Sox.

As further testament to the high esteem in which he was held, Joss was inducted into the Baseball Hall of Fame in 1978. Until that time he was ineligible for the Hall of Fame because the rules stipulate that candidates for enshrinement must have played in the major leagues for 10 full seasons. Joss's career ended nine years and a little more than one month after the Cleveland team purchased for $500 his contract from Toledo of the (minor league) Western Association.

The Hall of Fame's Veterans Committee voted to waive the rule in Joss's case, sixty-eight years after he pitched his final game on July 10, 1910.

The first indication of Joss's impending illness occurred shortly before the 1911 season began. During an exhibition game in Chattanooga, Tennessee, Joss fainted on the bench and was briefly hospitalized. He was able to rejoin the team a few days later and all seemed well again.

But soon Joss took sick again. He returned to his home in Toledo where his illness was diagnosed as tubercular meningitis, and within a week Joss died. It devastated his teammates and baseball fans alike.

Shortly thereafter, prior to Cleveland's scheduled season opener in Detroit—which was postponed in deference to Joss's grieving family and teammates—and funeral services were held in Toledo. A while later some of the top players in the American League formed an all-star team to play the Indians in an exhibition game. All of the proceeds were given to the widow of Joss, whose peak salary was $4,000 in 1907.

And so ended the Adrian "Addie" Joss era in Cleveland, an era in which Joss's fastball "seemed to be coming out of his hip pocket."

Ended, too, was an era that, because of Joss, might have been one of the greatest in Cleveland baseball history.

Year	Tm	W	L	ERA	GS	CG	SHO	IP	H	R	BB	SO
1902–1910	CLE (9 yrs.)	160	97	1.89	260	234	45	2327	1888	730	364	920

Stan Coveleski

Because he was "grandfathered" in the midst of his pitching career, Stan Coveleski's chances of reaching the Hall of Fame greatly improved.

Which, of course, might be an oversimplification because it also was Coveleski's dogged determination that played a large role in the realization of his dream.

Nicknamed the "Quiet Man" during his nine seasons with the Indians, Coveleski was one of 17 pitchers recognized as "legitimate spitballers" and, thus, were "grandfathered"—allowed to continue throwing the "unsavory" pitch—when baseball banned the spitball in 1920.

And 31 years after Coveleski retired in 1929 with a 215–142 won-lost record, he was elected to the Hall of Fame. Many of his victories were achieved because of his spitball, which Coveleski could make break three ways—down, out, or down and out. He also had outstanding control, in addition to an indomitable will to succeed.

It was the spitball that paved Coveleski's way to the Hall of Fame—as it also kept him in the major leagues after he had floundered in the minors from 1913 to 1915. The then-Philadelphia Athletics demoted him to Portland of the Pacific Coast League.

It was during his two-plus seasons in Portland that Coveleski learned to throw a spitball, and which, without a doubt, proved to be a career saver, as he seemingly was nearing the end in baseball when he was only 26.

With his newly learned spitball, Coveleski was acquired in 1916 by the Indians and won 15 games. He became the Indians' ace by 1918, the first of four consecutive seasons in which he won 20 games. In 1920, when his record was 24–14 and Cleveland won its first AL pennant, Coveleski became the first pitcher in major league baseball to win three games in the World Series, including the seventh against Brooklyn.

When his record began to decline in 1923, rumors circulated that Coveleski was "tipping off" his spitball, which still was his most effective pitch. After two more subpar seasons, and with Coveleski approaching the age of 36 after a 15–16 record in 1924, the Indians traded him to Washington for two soon-forgotten players. (For the record, they were Byron Speece, a pitcher, who won three games and lost five, and outfielder Carr Smith, who didn't play even one game for Cleveland.)

Coveleski went on to pitch effectively, posting a remarkable 20–5 record and 2.84 ERA in 1925 when the Senators won the AL pennant, although it turned out to be his last domineering season. His record slipped to 14–11 for the Senators in 1926, and arm problems hastened his retirement in 1927 when he won only two games. On June 17, 1927, the Polish spitballer was released.

In his 14-year major league career (which included two losing seasons for the New York Yankees), Coveleski pitched 224 complete games and an equally remarkable 3,082 innings. He also pitched more than 300 innings a season three times and more than 200 innings eight times.

Despite his reputation as a "quiet man," Coveleski spoke with impact during his Hall of Fame induction, which came 45 years after his final game on August 3, 1928, and 15 years prior to his death at age 94 in 1984. Still choosing his words carefully, Coveleski said, "I'd love to be pitching today with the stuff we had back when I pitched. Today they only use three pitches. We had six—spitball, curve ball, fastball, screwball, shine ball and emery ball."

But still, it was only one pitch, the spitball—a *legitimate* spitball, along with his dogged determination—that paved the way for Coveleski to make it to the Hall of Fame.

Year	Tm	W	L	ERA	GS	CG	SHO	IP	H	R	BB	SO
1916–1924	CLE (9 yrs)	172	123	2.80	305	194	31	2502	2450	972	616	856
1912	PHA (1 yr)	2	1	3.43	2	2	1	21	18	9	4	9
1925–1927	WSH (3 yrs)	36	17	2.98	70	26	6	500	515	205	162	111
1928	NYY (1 yr)	5	1	5.74	8	2	0	58	72	41	20	5
Total		215	142	2.89	385	224	38	3082	3055	1227	802	981

George Uhle

When he was a teenager in Rocky River, Ohio, a suburb of Cleveland in the early 1900s, George Uhle was a great fan of the Indians. Uhle, then playing on the sandlots of Cleveland as a pitcher, dreamed of playing for his favorite team (the Indians, of course) and winning 200 games in the major leagues.

As a 19 year old fresh out of high school in 1918, Uhle launched both of those dreams while pitching for the best amateur team in the city. It was sponsored by a company called Cleveland Standard Parts. Subsequently, when Uhle helped Cleveland Standard Parts win not just the Cleveland or even the United States amateur baseball championship but the *world* amateur baseball championship, the first part of his two dreams became reality.

Three teams tried to sign Uhle, but only one prevailed—the Indians. And soon thereafter Uhle began a 19-year major league career, which led to the second part of Uhle's goal.

In 1919, without spending even one day in the minor leagues, Uhle pitched and won 10 games as an Indians rookie, often working in relief of two of the pitchers he'd admired, Jim Bagby and Stan Coveleski.

He was 16–13 in 1921, a 20-game winner (with 16 losses) in 1922, and became the AL's winningest pitcher (26–16) in 1923. Uhle also led the league with 27 victories (11 losses) in 1926, and he went on to post a 147–119 record for the Indians through 1928.

(Editor's note: Uhle is included in the 1901–25 era of Indians because his success started during that time, though he continued to pitch for the Tigers, Yankees, and New York Giants before his retirement in 1936.)

Among his credentials: Uhle was considered one of the smartest pitchers of his time, a factor that undoubtedly was based on his success against Babe Ruth.

Uhle recalled Ruth's death in 1985: "Early in the Babe's career he hit a pop fly home run off me in the [New York] Polo Grounds, but he never got another [homer] off me until after I was traded to Detroit. The way I pitched to Ruth, I'd give him a lot of slow breaking stuff, then try to blow a fastball by him. None of the great hitters like slow stuff because it throws off their timing. They all want to hit fastballs."

Apparently Uhle's strategy was correct because Ruth once called Uhle the best he ever faced. Uhle also is credited with introducing a new pitch. He called it a "slider," and named it as such when describing the motion of the pitch. "It's something like a fastball but not as fast, and something like a curveball, but doesn't break as much." Others sneeringly referred to it as a "nickel curve," but Uhle stuck with it—which might have been a reason he was nicknamed "The Bull." And now the slider is one of the most used—and most effective—pitches by the best pitchers in baseball.

Uhle also was considered one of the best hitters in baseball and often was used as a pinch hitter. In fact, once he batted for Tris Speaker, though he "couldn't recall" the details.

Uhle pitched for the Tigers from 1928 to 1933, the Giants and Yankees also in 1933, and retired after the 1934 season with the Yankees—but not until he won two of his six pitching decisions in 10 games. That is, two victories for 200, and a lifetime 200–166 won-lost record, fulfilling another of the goals Uhle dreamed of reaching when it all began on the Cleveland sandlots 15 years earlier.

Year	Tm	W	L	ERA	GS	CG	SHO	IP	H	R	BB	SO
1919–28, 1936	CLE (11yrs)	147	119	3.92	267	166	16	2200	2442	1137	709	763
1929–1933	DET (5 yrs)	44	41	3.91	92	62	5	828	866	425	224	332
1933–1934	NYY (2 yrs)	8	5	6.17	8	4	0	77	93	61	27	36
1933	NYG (1 yr)	1	1	7.90	1	0	0	13	16	12	6	4
Total		200	166	3.99	368	232	21	3119	3417	1635	966	1135

Joe Jackson

As long as the game is played, there probably will be questions about "Shoeless Joe" Jackson, one of the best players to ever wear a Cleveland uniform—albeit if only briefly—as to whether he should have been banned from baseball for life.

The speculation is based on Jackson's alleged guilt and involvement with seven of his Chicago White Sox teammates who allegedly conspired with gamblers to intentionally lose the 1919 World Series to the Cincinnati Reds.

Those who insist that Jackson was not part of the conspiracy to let the National League champion Reds win five games cite Jackson's record in the Series. He made 12 hits and batted .375, the highest average of all the players in the eight games (which then comprised the World Series) and didn't commit an error or blatant misplay.

Rumors of the dishonesty of the White Sox were the first test of the new commissioner's authority. Kenesaw Mountain Landis took his time reaching a decision, but finally, in 1921, Landis banned the players from baseball for life, even though all—including Jackson—had been acquitted in 1920 by a Chicago grand jury.

White Sox owner Charles Comiskey apparently was not in agreement with Landis. Comiskey was quoted as saying, "I think [Landis] wanted to make an impact on the game. He wanted his owners and players to know, 'Hey, I'm the boss. I'm the supreme commander.'" Maybe so.

Landis, previously a federal judge, was hired by the baseball club owners and charged with reestablishing the fans' confidence in the integrity of major league baseball.

Another who questioned the severity of Landis's decision—at least the inclusion of Jackson as part of the conspiracy—was venerable Philadelphia Athletics owner and manager Connie Mack. He commented, "I always thought that he [Jackson] was more sinned against than sinning."

Whatever the case, there's no doubt about Jackson's greatness as a player. In his 13-plus seasons in the major leagues, Jackson's career batting average was .356, the third highest of any player already in the Hall of Fame.

Jackson, who was said to have been "illiterate," admitted having knowledge of the conspiracy, which obviously strengthened Landis's decision to throw him out of baseball.

Reportedly, Jackson was initially approached by gamblers and offered $5,000 up front and $15,000 later to join the players who had agreed to throw the Series. Jackson was said to have refused the $5,000, claiming that one of his teammates took the money and left it in his room. It was not returned to the gamblers—but neither was the final $15,000 payment ever made to Jackson.

Jackson's strongest denial of any wrongdoing was in a statement he made long after he'd been barred by Landis: "God knows I gave my best in baseball at all times, and no man on earth can truthfully judge me otherwise."

Jackson's major league baseball career began in Philadelphia in 1908. Acquired by the Indians in 1910, Jackson played only briefly his first year in Cleveland before bursting into stardom.

In 1911, in 147 games, he hit .408, and he still is only one of six players to hit .400 in one season. Ironically, Jackson's .408 average was only second best in the AL, as Cobb won the 1911 batting title with a .420 average.

And, thus, the speculation persists. Was he or was he not involved in the conspiracy? And should he be eligible for the Hall of Fame? One thing that cannot be doubted: Jackson's ability to play the game as well as—if not better than—anyone then or since his final game on September 27, 1920.

His batting average that season was .382. Unfortunately, it wasn't for the Indians.

Year	Tm	G	AB	R	H	HR	RBI	SB	BB	SO	BA
1910–1915	CLE (6 yrs)	674	2502	474	937	24	353	138	267	141	.375
1908–1909	PHA (2 yrs)	10	40	3	6	0	6	0	1	6	.150
1915–1920	CHW (6 yrs)	648	2439	396	829	30	426	64	251	87	.340
Total		1332	4981	873	1772	54	785	202	519	234	.356

Steve O'Neill

There's no plaque, not even a photograph of Steve O'Neill is displayed prominently in the Hall of Fame, but there's little doubt that the genial Irishman deserves more recognition than he's generally given.

Not only was O'Neill a very good (if under-publicized) player of his time, he was also a teammate of many of the Indians' all-time greats and a contemporary of other Hall of Famers.

O'Neill was behind the plate for the Indians for 13 of his 17 seasons (1911–28) in the major leagues, and managed four teams (Cleveland, Detroit, Boston Red Sox, and Philadelphia Phillies). Of even greater significance, O'Neill was one of a very select few who played for and managed teams that won the World Series: the Indians in 1920 and Tigers in 1945.

If he had a fault, as some have said, it probably could best be stated by repeating a headline that appeared in the *Cleveland News* atop a story by prominent sports columnist Ed McAuley. "Get Mad, Steve! Get Mad!" the headline screamed across the sports pages over McAuley's open letter admonishing O'Neill in 1937 as the Indians were in the midst of losing 13 of 15 games.

It apparently convinced Indians owner Alva Bradley to fire O'Neill when the Indians ended the season in fourth place, 19 games behind the pennant-winning New York Yankees.

O'Neill, undaunted by either McAuley's criticism or the blame by Bradley, went back to the minor leagues where he managed Toronto and later Buffalo in the International League for the next five years. Then, apparently after getting "mad" enough, O'Neill was hired by Detroit where he managed the Tigers from 1943 to 1948, including 1945 when they won the pennant.

O'Neill went on to manage the Boston Red Sox from 1950 to 1951 and the Philadelphia Phillies from 1952 to 1954. He also served as a coach for the Indians, Tigers, and Red Sox on various occasions. O'Neill retired at age 63 and died eight years later on January 25, 1962. He was lauded by many, including McAuley, for being "a genuinely good guy."

There's no question that O'Neill was genuinely good enough during his major league playing career beginning on August 11, 1911, when he was claimed in the minor league draft from the Philadelphia Athletics. He continued in Cleveland for the next 12 years, hitting .300 or better three times (1920–22), and he was one of the Indians' leaders in 1920 when they won their first pennant and World Series. That was O'Neill's best season as he batted .321 in 149 games.

O'Neill's lifetime batting average was .263 in 1,586 games. He was behind the plate for the Indians in 1,335 games, including all seven in the 1920 World Series. Only Jim Hegan caught more games (1,491) for the Tribe.

Also impressive is O'Neill's won-lost record as a major league manager: 1,040–821 (.559). He never had a losing record in 14 seasons at the helm of the Indians, Tigers, Red Sox, or Phillies.

He was highly respected for his leadership as a minor league manager and is generally credited for developing Lou Boudreau and Bob Feller with the Indians, as well as a the volatile and temperamental Hal Newhouser with the Tigers and Robin Roberts with the Phillies. All four are in the Hall of Fame.

After O'Neill retired, McAuley, despite his previous criticism of O'Neill, wrote: "[O'Neill] played with one world championship club and managed another. Not many men in all the history of the game have been as lucky—if that's the word for it—as O'Neill has been, and no one begrudges him his happy fortune.

"Stephen Francis O'Neill is one of the genuinely good guys of our time."

Year	Tm	G	AB	R	H	HR	RBI	SB	BB	SO	BA
1911–1923	CLE (13 yrs)	1365	4182	394	1109	11	458	30	491	382	.265
1924	BOS (1 yr)	106	307	29	73	0	38	0	63	23	.238
1925	NYY (1 yr)	35	91	7	26	1	13	0	10	3	.286
1927–1928	SLB (2 yrs)	84	215	18	51	1	28	0	28	6	.237
Total		1590	4795	448	1259	13	537	30	592	414	.263

Napoleon "Nap" Lajoie

Napoleon Lajoie was so great a player for the Cleveland baseball club in the early days of the American League—and so popular, too—that the nickname of the team was officially changed to honor him, by vote of the fans in 1904.

The *Cleveland Press* ran a "re-naming" referendum and "Naps" won, in recognition of Lajoie's outstanding ability and personality as the team's manager and second baseman.

Until then the Cleveland team was known as "Bronchos" in 1902 and 1903, and previously "Blues" in 1901. When Lajoie resigned as the manager in 1909, fans were polled again to choose another nickname. This time the favorite was "Indians," allegedly (though often disputed) to honor a former player whose pre-1901 deeds with the old Cleveland Spiders were remembered. This player was Louis Sockalexis, an American Indian who had been a star on the Cleveland team that played in the National League in the 1890s.

Lajoie was one of the best players in the AL, and he took over as manager four years after joining Cleveland in 1902, and led it to fifth-, fourth-, and second-place finishes, narrowly missing winning the pennant in 1908.

Lajoie resigned as manager in August of 1909, though he remained as a player through 1914, after which his contract was sold to the Philadelphia Athletics.

During his 13 seasons with the team that used his name as a nickname, Lajoie—whose top salary was $12,000 in each of his final three years with the Naps—batted .300 or better 10 times. His average was .344 and .376 back-to-back when he led the AL in 1903 and 1904, and .384 in 1910 when he won his third batting title.

Lajoie's return to the Athletics in 1915 was a matter of déjà vu and provided another twist in the career of the 40-year-old second baseman as he began in Philadelphia with the Phillies in 1896.

In 1901, the newly formed American League included a Philadelphia team, the Athletics, as a new local rival of the Phillies. Lajoie, who couldn't get the raise he wanted from the Phillies, chose to jump to the Athletics. In his first season with the Athletics he won the AL batting championship with a .426 average.

The Phillies tried to force Lajoie to return by filing a lawsuit. It went to the Pennsylvania Supreme Court, which returned a restraining order against Lajoie, forbidding him from playing baseball for any team in Pennsylvania except the Phillies.

That's when Connie Mack, owner of the Athletics, repaid what had been a financial favor to Charles Somers, owner of the Cleveland team. Mack ostensibly "gave" Lajoie to Cleveland for $25,000, though sources claimed that no money was involved.

However, the gift, while welcomed by the Cleveland team, still prevented Lajoie from playing in Pennsylvania for any team except the Phillies, and the ruling had no jurisdiction over Lajoie outside the state. Thus, Lajoie was able to resume his burgeoning career with Cleveland but never in a game in Philadelphia—or anywhere in Pennsylvania. The injunction died a natural death in 1906, when Lajoie was able to play a full season for the first time in the AL.

After Lajoie's contract was sold back to the Philadelphia Athletics in 1915, he played two more years and then another two more in the minor leagues before finally retiring at age 44. He died in 1959 at age 84.

His career batting average for 21 seasons was .338, and in 1936 Lajoie was elected to the Hall of Fame in only the second year of its existence, preceded by only five players to be so honored: Ty Cobb, Walter Johnson, Christy Mathewson, Babe Ruth, and Honus Wagner.

Year	Tm	G	AB	R	H	HR	RBI	SB	BB	SO	BA
1902–1914	CLE (13 yrs)	1614	6034	865	2046	33	919	240	408	221	.339
1896–1900	PHI (5 yrs)	492	2091	421	721	32	458	87	59	74	.345
1901, 1902, 1915, 1916	PHA (4 yrs)	374	1464	218	475	17	222	53	49	51	.324
Total		2480	9589	1504	3242	82	1599	380	516	346	.338

Jim Bagby Sr.

It is a generally accepted assumption that pitchers who win 300 games and batters who make 3,000 hits in their careers automatically become prime candidates for election to the Baseball Hall of Fame. Another oft-considered qualification—though certainly not an absolute pass into the hallowed Hall—are pitchers who win 30 games in one season. The only pitcher who did it and, hence, flirted with baseball immortality while wearing a Cleveland uniform but never came close again, was right-hander Jim Bagby Sr., aka "Ol' Sarge," in 1920.

His record that season was 31–12 with a 2.89 ERA, establishing him as the only Tribe pitcher to win more than the 27 games Bob Feller did in 1940. In so doing, Bagby led the Indians to the pennant and World Series championship, although he could not sustain his success in subsequent seasons.

Bagby's seven-season record with the Indians was 122–86, obviously not Hall of Fame numbers, and two years after helping to write World Series history Bagby was gone. His career careened downhill after he was let go by the Indians to Pittsburgh in a waiver deal in 1922.

In fact, it might have been his heavy-duty workload in 1920 that caused Bagby's early demise, just as it was his remarkable performances under pressure that led the Tribe to its first pennant.

Bagby won his first eight decisions in 1920, and by late June his record was 14–2. On July 19 he pitched in both games of a doubleheader, beating Boston in the opener with 2⅔ innings of one-hit, no-run relief. He then started the second game and took a 4–2 lead into the eighth inning when he tired and the Indians eventually lost. The next day Bagby entered a tie game in the eighth inning, gave up one run,

and won in the eleventh inning. Equally remarkable was that late in July of 1920 his record was 20–5.

Bagby slumped to 14–12 in 1921, then to 4–5 in 1922, and he pitched only two more seasons in the major leagues, for Pittsburgh in 1923 and for Cincinnati in 1924.

It is no exaggeration to say that had Bagby not been so successful in 1920, the Indians would not have been successful either. They finished the season only two games ahead of the defending (and disgraced) 1919 World Series champion Chicago White Sox.

Many have speculated that the Indians prevailed primarily because eight Chicago players were suspended—subsequently permanently from baseball—with four games left in the 1920 season. It was then that commissioner Kenesaw Mountain Landis charged them with intentionally losing to Cincinnati in the 1919 World Series.

Landis issued his suspension of the players with four games remaining in the 1920 season. And, without those eight players, the White Sox lost three of their final four games, while the Indians won three of their last five to capture the AL pennant with a 98–56 record, two lengths ahead of the second-place White Sox.

Bagby retired with a 127–89 record after nine-plus major league seasons as—early on—one of the most promising pitchers in baseball. But, for whatever reason, he was unable to sustain his success and by 1924 was back on his farm in Georgia. He died in 1954 at the age of 65.

Indeed, perhaps it was all those pitches Bagby threw in 1920 that took its toll on his arm and eventually led to the premature demise of his once-promising pitching career. But still, those 31 victories in 1920 will always stand as a lasting monument to Jim Bagby Sr. in the annals of Cleveland baseball history—and to what might have been.

Indians	W	L	Pct	ERA	G	CG	IP	H	BB	SO	ShO
1916	16	16	.500	2.61	48	14	272.2	253	67	88	3
1917	23	13	.639	1.96	49	26	320.2	277	73	83	8
1918	17	16	.515	2.69	45	23	271.1	274	78	57	2
1919	17	11	.607	2.80	35	21	241.1	258	44	61	0
1920	31	12	.721	2.89	48	30	339.2	338	79	73	3
1921	14	12	.538	4.70	40	13	191.2	238	44	37	0
1922	4	5	.444	6.32	25	4	98.1	134	39	25	0
Career	127	88	.591	3.11	316	133	1,821.2	1,884	458	450	16

Tris Speaker

When the Indians made one of their all-time best deals— the acquisition of Tris Speaker—one person was very angry. —Tris Speaker

Speaker "absolutely" refused to come to Cleveland primarily because, he said, the team had a legacy as losers. He said he even hated to come to the city as a visiting player. Money, of course, was a defining issue, but to Speaker another negative factor was his desire to continue playing for the Red Sox in Boston.

By then, during the winter of 1915–16, Speaker had become an icon in Boston, compiling a cumulative .337 average in eight-plus seasons after joining the Red Sox as a rookie in 1907. He led the team to the American League pennant and World Series championship in 1915 when he batted .322.

The money also became a factor when the owner of the Red Sox, Joe Lannin, wanted Speaker to sign a contract calling for him to be paid $9,000 for 1916, the same salary he was paid in 1915. The offer was justified, Lannin claimed, because Speaker's average had declined in each of the preceding four seasons from a high of .383 in 1912 (when he won the AL Most Valuable Player award). Speaker batted .363 in 1913, .338 in 1914, and .327 in 1915.

But Speaker was adamant in his demand for a $6,000 raise, while the Red Sox were equally adamant in their rejection.

That's when a Cleveland sportswriter, Ed Bang of the *Cleveland News,* learned the details of the salary impasse. He suggested to Bob McKoy, then general manager of the Indians, that they try to make a deal for Speaker.

McKoy took Bang's advice and offered $35,000 and two players, pitcher Sad Sam Jones and infielder Fred Thomas, for Speaker.

Lannin agreed and the trade was trumpeted as one that would be the "biggest deal in baseball."

But it didn't appease Speaker, who still refused unless Lannin pay him $10,000 of the $35,000 the Red Sox were receiving from the Indians.

Lannin refused, saying he would never pay a player to approve a trade. Then American League president Ban Johnson stepped in and convinced Lannin to make the deal and pay Speaker the money he wanted.

And so the Indians obtained the player who would become one of their all-time best—perhaps *the* best— who would take the franchise to its first pennant and World Series championship in 1920, in exchange for two fringe players.

Speaker, aka the "Gray Eagle," who played a unique short center field—and who admittedly learned to "love" the city he previously "hated" and the team that had a legacy for losing—soon was idolized by adoring fans in return.

Speaker became the Indians' player-manager in mid-1919 and continued at the helm for a total of eight years through 1926, finishing second three times and batting .300 or better in 10 of his 11 seasons in Cleveland, including a league-leading .386 in 1916.

Speaker left the Indians as a free agent following the 1926 season. In 1927 he played for Washington where he hit .300 (.327) for the last time, and in 1928 he played part-time for the Philadelphia Athletics.

The one-time Gray Eagle retired with a major league career total of 3,514 hits, ranking fifth in baseball history. In 1937 Speaker became the seventh player elected to the Hall of Fame, after only Ty Cobb, Walter Johnson, Christy Mathewson, Babe Ruth, Honus Wagner, and Napoleon Lajoie.

Speaker, who died in 1958 at age 70, returned to Cleveland in the late 1940s as a part-time coach and later did some part-time broadcasting.

And, for the record, he no longer hated to play—or work—in Cleveland.

Year	Tm	G	AB	R	H	HR	RBI	SB	BB	SO	BA
1916–1926	CLE(11 yrs)	1519	5546	1079	1965	73	884	155	857	146	.354
1907–1915	BOS (9 yrs)	1065	3935	704	1327	39	542	267	459	236	.337
1927	WSH (1 yr)	141	523	71	171	2	73	9	55	8	.327
1928	PHA (1 yr)	64	191	28	51	3	30	5	10	5	.267
Total		2789	10195	1882	3514	117	1529	436	1381	395	.345

Joey Sewell

Quickly now: what batter in major league baseball history holds the record for strikeouts, which undoubtedly helped get him elected to the Hall of Fame?

No, not the *most* strikeouts in one season.

The fewest.

The answer: Joey Sewell—and it's easy to speculate that the Indians probably would not have won their first pennant and World Series in 1920 if not for him.

Sewell's remarkable story is that, not only did he make it to the hallowed Hall in Cooperstown in 1977, but that it was literally an accident that he made it as far as Cleveland.

Sewell, in 1920, was a 21-year-old kid shortstop from the University of Alabama who'd never played more than 30 games, nor batted more than 100 times in professional baseball as a rookie shortstop at New Orleans of the Class A Southern Association.

It was almost as a last resort that the Indians called Sewell to help keep alive their dwindling pennant chances on September 6, 1920, when their hopes of clinging to first place in the American League were very slim. Only three weeks earlier, on August 17, 1920, their problems worsened when they lost their spark plug shortstop, Ray Chapman.

As most fans know, Chapman is the only player in major league history to have been killed playing the game: he was hit in the left temple by a pitch thrown by the New York Yankees' Carl Mays.

Harry Lunte, a utility infielder, was initially tried at shortstop, but a week later suffered an injury that sidelined him. Then, Doc Evans, a converted outfielder, was shifted to shortstop but soon was found wanting. So, Indians owner James Dunn and manager Tris Speaker, growing ever more desperate, turned to the minor leagues and acquired Sewell.

As Dunn admitted then, there was considerable doubt as to whether Sewell could fill Lunte's shoes, let alone those worn by Chapman. But the Indians had no chance of getting anybody better to play the key position that would help keep them in first place.

As Speaker admitted, the Indians had no choice. "We have to gamble on anything now," he said about choosing Sewell.

And so Sewell was promoted to Cleveland—and how fortunate it turned out to be, for him and the Indians.

Sewell batted .329, and he even drove in 12 runs and scored 14 in the Tribe's remaining 22 games. Though he was charged with 15 errors, he made most of the big plays that helped keep the Indians atop the AL and ahead of the Chicago White Sox.

And, after he helped the Indians win the pennant and World Series against Brooklyn, Sewell went on to be an Indians mainstay for the next ten years. Sewell, who died in 1990 at age 91, played in the major leagues for 14 years, signing as a free agent with the New York Yankees in 1931 and helping them reach the World Series in 1933.

And, while batting a cumulative .320, including .300 nine times—with a high of .353 in 1923—he hit 49 homers in his career and led the Indians in RBI three times.

There also was something else very unusual—even unique about Joey Sewell, which goes back to the top of this story. That is, Sewell struck out a hard-to-believe *total* of only 114 times in 1,903 major league games. In 1930, he fanned three times in 109 games!

Compare Sewell's numbers with the strikeouts compiled by players currently in the major leagues: Mark Reynolds of Arizona (and now the 2013 Indians) led them all with 223 in 2009.

And, the way today's game is played—and is progressing—makes it unlikely that Sewell's record will ever be broken.

Year	Tm	G	AB	R	H	HR	RBI	SB	BB	SO	BA
1920–1930	CLE (11 yrs)	1513	5621	857	1800	30	869	71	654	99	.320
1931–1933	NYY (3 yrs)	390	1511	284	426	19	186	3	188	15	.282
Total		1903	7132	1141	2226	49	1055	74	842	114	.312

Elmer Flick

If it happened today it would become one of the biggest stories of the year, headlined and debated incessantly on radio and television talk shows.

It was in the spring of 1908 when Charles Somers, owner of the Naps franchise in the infant American League, said "thanks but no thanks" to the Detroit Tigers' offer to trade Ty Cobb to Cleveland for outfielder Elmer Flick.

Imagine how different the fortunes of the Cleveland and Detroit teams would have evolved if Somers had said yes. Flick, a native Clevelander and a favorite of the fans, had hit .302 in 1907 and won the American League batting championship in 1905. Cobb, on the other hand, the reigning AL batting champion in 1907, only his first full season in the major leagues, had a much different persona. He was not well liked by either fans or teammates.

However, despite his personality, Cobb was a winning player as he dominated baseball for most of the next 20 years before retiring in 1928 with a career batting average of .366, the best in major league baseball history.

Except for his first year in 1905 when he appeared in only 41 games, Cobb never hit less than .300, including .420 in 1911 and .410 in 1912. He won 10 batting championships and was the first player elected to the Hall of Fame in 1936. But in the spring of 1908, few of Cobb's pluses were present when the Tigers decided they wanted a "harmonious" teammate instead of Cobb. The conversation between Charles Somers and Hughie Jennings, manager of the Tigers, went like this, according to newspaper accounts of the day:

"We want to rid our team of Cobb," Jennings told Somers.

"Why?" asked Somers. "Is there anything wrong with Cobb?"

Jennings replied, "[Cobb] is in good health. But we don't want him on our team because

he cannot get along with our players. We want harmony on this team, not scrapping."

"Well, we want harmony, too," Somers said, and thanked Jennings.

But in today's win-at-any-cost attitude, so prevalent in professional sports, it's unlikely any team would unload its best player because he was a "scrapper."

Flick went on to complete a Hall of Fame career in 1910, compiling a lifetime batting average of .313.

Although relatively anonymous to today's fans, he was one of the great all-around players at the turn of the century and a star for the Philadelphia Phillies of the National League from 1898–1901.

In 1902, one year after the American League was founded, Flick and two Phillies teammates, Napoleon Lajoie and Wilson Bernhard, jumped their contracts to join the Cleveland team. However, they were stopped by an injunction obtained by the Phillies, preventing them from playing for any team outside the state of Pennsylvania.

They signed with the Philadelphia Athletics, one of the new AL franchises, and two weeks into the 1903 season Connie Mack, owner-manager of the Athletics and a close friend of Somers, dealt all three to Cleveland.

As long as the former Phillies did not play any games in Pennsylvania, the injunction didn't have any effect on them. (It eventually died when the NL and AL made peace in 1903.)

Flick played for Cleveland into the 1910 season when stomach problems forced him into retirement at age 34 with a career batting average of .313. He was elected to the Hall of Fame in 1963 and died in 1971 at age 95.

And though neither Flick's career average nor any of his best years matched those of Cobb, there may have been some consolation in the fact that they were achieved on a team where "harmony" prevailed—even if the won-lost record would have been preferable.

Year	Tm	G	AB	R	H	HR	RBI	SB	BB	SO	BA
1902–1910	CLE (9 yrs)	935	3537	535	1058	19	376	207	355	410	.299
1898–1901	PHI (4 yrs)	537	2023	400	683	29	377	119	236	153	.338
1902	PHA (1 yr)	11	37	15	11	0	3	4	6	2	.297
Total		1483	5597	950	1752	48	756	330	597	565	.313

1926–1950

Mel Harder

Mel Harder is not in the Hall of Fame, though many believe he *should* be—just as they also are puzzled as to why he isn't already among the game's immortals. Their rationale is based primarily on the fact that Harder's 223 victories are more than the number of games won by 17 of the 56 starting pitchers already enshrined. Harder's victories (with 186 losses) over 20 seasons also are the second most by an Indians pitcher to only Bob Feller.

Harder was the first Indians pitcher to win 200 games and the first to make 500 appearances; he is still the all-time leader in games pitched (582). He was a 20-game winner twice, in 1934 (20–12) and 1935 (22–11) and won 15 or more games eight times.

And finally in support of his credentials for election to the Hall of Fame: two of the current members might not be there if they had not been tutored by Harder—Early Wynn and Bob Lemon. Both developed under Harder when he was the Tribe pitching coach. Harder also was instrumental in the development of other young pitchers, namely Herb Score, Mike Garcia, Mudcat Grant, and Gary Bell. And even when ageless Satchel Paige joined the Indians in 1948, Harder also was available as a tutor—although, as Harder once recalled, "Satch probably could've taught me a few things."

Harder's pitching career with the Indians, the only team whose uniform he wore as a player from 1928 to 1947, was very good until he suffered arm problems. His prime seasons were in the mid-1930s to the early 1940s, which coincided with the some of the best years of two of baseball's greatest sluggers, Joe DiMaggio and Ted Williams. Both were outspoken in their praise of Harder. DiMaggio, whose career batting average was .325 (but only .180 in games against Harder), called him the best pitcher he ever faced.

And Williams, in his autobiography, *My Turn at Bat,* said "Harder had a great curve ball, great control, and every one of his pitches did something different."

Before he died in 2002 at age 93, Harder spoke of his biggest thrill—the game he pitched on July 31, 1932. It was the first played in the new Cleveland Municipal Stadium and was against the Philadelphia Athletics. More than 80,000 fans were there. "It was the biggest thrill of my baseball career to pitch in front of all those people. I would've liked to win [the Athletics did, 1–0] but I wasn't any more disappointed than any game I lost."

In that historic opener against Lefty Grove, Harder allowed five hits, and in the sixth inning struck out in succession three future Hall of Famers, Mickey Cochrane, Al Simmons, and Jimmie Foxx.

Another performance Harder could have recounted was the first of his four consecutive All-Star games (1934–37). He still is the only pitcher to work a total of 13 innings without allowing a run. Harder became the winning pitcher in the 1934 game by shutting out the National Leaguers on one hit through the final five innings. It was the game in which the NL's Carl Hubbell struck out five future Hall of Famers in succession—Babe Ruth, Lou Gehrig, Jimmie Foxx, Al Simmons, and Joe Cronin—and received most of the accolades for his performance.

And so, because of the passage of time and the number of ballots that have been counted without Harder winning what would seem to be his rightful plaque in the Hall of Fame, it's probably too late to hope for the best for Harder in future elections.

As has been said—and *should* be said again—baseball, like life, is not always fair.

Year	Tm	W	L	ERA	GS	CG	SHO	IP	H	R	BB	SO
1928–47	CLE(20 yrs)	223	186	3.80	582	181	25	3426	3706	1714	1118	1161

Bob Feller

A one-dollar signing bonus? That and an autographed baseball are all it took to sign a 16-year-old high school kid—one who would become an Indians icon and one of the best pitchers of all time. Perhaps even *the* best.

A few months after the 1935 acquisition, the Indians were fined $7,500 because commissioner Kenesaw Mountain Landis decreed they broke a rule then in effect by promoting Feller to the major leagues without his having pitched in the minor leagues. Not only did Landis fine the Indians but he also ordered that Feller be "freed," making him eligible to sign with any team. But Feller and his dad said no. "I want to pitch for the Indians. Mr. [scout C. C.] Slapnicka was honest and fair and we want to be honest and fair, too. We made a good faith agreement just as they did," said Feller.

The autographed ball, Feller's canceled bonus check (dated July 22, 1935), and a copy of his agreement with the Indians are on display in Feller's museum in Van Meter, Iowa.

"When Landis wanted to void my contract it angered my dad who always insisted his word was his bond. I felt the same," said Feller.

Because he was still in high school, Feller attended classes and his graduation, commuting between Cleveland and Van Meter in 1935 and early 1936, during which he pitched for a local amateur team.

Feller faced a major league hitter for the first time on July 19, 1936, in an exhibition game against the Washington Senators. His first appearance in a regulation game was against Detroit on August 23, 1936. Feller struck out 15 and won, 4–1.

Elected to the Hall of Fame in 1962, Feller pitched 570 games, the most in Tribe history and finished on September 30, 1956, with a career record of 266–162.

Among the victories were three no-hitters: one against the Chicago White Sox on April 16, 1940, 1–0, the only Opening Day no-hitter in baseball history; another against New York, 1–0, in 1946; and the final in Detroit, 2–1, in 1951.

He also pitched 12 one-hitters, won 20 games six times, set the single-season strikeout record of 348 in 1946, and fanned 2,581 batters in 3,827 innings. Two other statistics of pride to Feller: he pitched more than 300 innings three times, including an AL high 371 in 1946; he pitched 200 innings 10 times; and he completed 279 of the 484 games he started in his 18 seasons.

Feller also was a national hero. In 1941, on December 10, three days after the Japanese bombed Pearl Harbor, Feller enlisted in the Navy. He served 44 months as a gunnery mate aboard the USS *Alabama,* earning eight battle stars, and resumed his baseball career late in 1945. It has been estimated that Feller would have won as many as 100 more games had he not lost 3½ seasons in World War II.

But Feller insisted he had few regrets before his 2010 death at age 93. "I am sorry we didn't win more pennants, especially when we came so close in 1940; and that I didn't win a World Series game [in 1948 he lost, 1–0, on what was later acknowledged to be a blown call by an umpire; the other reference, Game 5 in 1948, was an 11–5 loss]. I also regret I didn't get a chance to pitch in the 1954 World Series. There might be others, but they really aren't important. But I never regretted leaving my career and serving my country in World War II. And I never regretted that I signed with the Indians and didn't go with anyone else when Landis said I could."

Even though his signing "bonus" was only a dollar and an autographed baseball.

Year	Tm	W	L	ERA	GS	CG	SHO	IP	H	R	BB	SO
1936–56	CLE (18 yrs)	266	162	3.25	484	279	44	3827	3271	1557	1764	2581

Earl Averill

It was the winter of 1928–29 and Indians general manager Billy Evans met with owner Alva Bradley to introduce the team's newest player. He was a 28-year-old outfielder named Earl Averill whose contract was acquired from the San Francisco Seals of the Class AAA Pacific Coast League for $40,000 and two minor leaguers.

Reportedly, the owner forced a smile and said he was glad to meet his new player.

But when the door closed, Bradley—normally an easygoing gentleman—suddenly was not so gentlemanly. "You mean we paid all that money for a midget?" Bradley demanded.

Averill, the "midget," who subsequently was listed on the Tribe roster as being five foot nine, a left-handed hitting center fielder, would play for the Indians the next 11 seasons.

Shortly after that initial meeting, Averill reignited Bradley's ire by refusing to play unless the Indians paid him a bonus. "If I am worth $40,000 [to the Seals], I am worth $5,000 to myself," he argued.

A peace treaty was struck and Averill went on to bat .332 as a rookie, immediately winning over the fans.

In his first at-bat against Detroit in the 1929 opener, Averill became the first player to hit a home run in his first trip to the plate. He went on to hit 18 homers and drive in 96 runs that season.

The fans loved Averill, even though the front office didn't—primarily because he seldom failed to speak his mind.

But he proved his worth on the field. Averill hit .300-plus in his first six seasons. His average dropped to .288 in 1935 because—in the opinion of his teammate Mel Harder—Averill played the final six weeks with a badly burned hand, the result of an accident. The mishap occurred when Averill was "playing around with some high-powered firecrackers at a team picnic on the Fourth of July," Harder said.

In 1936 Averill rebounded to hit .378—with an AL leading 232 hits—of which 28 were homers. That was the year Luke Appling of Chicago won the batting championship with a .388 average, which led to another rift between Averill and the Indians front office.

Because he came so close to winning the batting title, Averill demanded a $2,000 raise over his $14,000 salary.

Bradley was outraged. But finally another peace treaty was reached, this one granting Averill a $1,000 raise and a $2,000 bonus, provided he had what Bradley would deem a "good" year in 1937.

Averill didn't have a good year, at least not in the opinion of Bradley. So once again the two men disagreed. Bradley insisted that Averill batted "only" .299, just the second time in his 11 seasons that he hit less than .300, which still wasn't good enough for Bradley, who refused to pay Averill the bonus.

But the fans remained in Averill's corner, rewarding him with what star players of that era used to get—a "day." Averill was showered with gifts, and, in addition to money, received a new Cadillac.

Averill had another good year in 1938—even Bradley had to agree–with a .330 average, but still was sent packing. On June 14, 1939, shortly after he turned 37 and was batting .273, partly because of ongoing leg problems, Averill was traded to Detroit for pitcher Harry Eisenstat and cash. Averill played two partial seasons in Detroit with mediocre success and attempted a comeback in 1941 with Boston but played only 10 games and was released.

And in 1975 the player Bradley called a "midget," who went on to fashion a .318 career batting average, was elected to the Hall of Fame. He died in 1983 at age 81.

Year	Tm	G	AB	R	H	HR	RBI	SB	BB	SO	BA
1929–1939	CLE (11 yrs)	1510	5909	1154	1903	226	1084	66	725	470	.322
1939–1940	DET (2 yrs)	151	427	68	114	12	78	4	48	44	.267
1941	BSN (1 yr)	8	17	2	2	0	2	0	1	4	.118
Total		1669	6353	1224	2019	238	1164	70	774	518	.318

Lou Boudreau

When Lou Boudreau was inducted into the Hall of Fame in 1970, he was introduced by Commissioner Bowie Kuhn who said of the former shortstop and manager of the Indians: "The most remarkable thing about this remarkable man was the way he stretched his wonderful skills into superlative skills," and that, "from all this he fashioned the wonderful ball player that we know as Lou Boudreau."

It was the perfect culmination to Boudeau's baseball career.

He joined the Indians as a 20-year-old youth fresh out of college in 1938, took over as their shortstop in 1939, became their player-manager in 1941 and won the American League batting championship in 1944. He also was the American League all-star shortstop eight times and the overwhelming winner of the AL's Most Valuable Player award in 1948 when he led the franchise through its most thrilling season to capture the pennant and World Series for the first time in 28 years, and only the second in club history.

Boudreau acknowledged Kuhn's plaudits with humility. "Those are memories I'll cherish forever," he said—as do fans of the Boudreau era and the golden years in Cleveland baseball history, including one in particular, going back to November 24, 1947. That's when Bill Veeck, who purchased the team in 1946, believed the Indians needed a new manager to replace Boudreau. However, to do so he realized he had to acquire a new shortstop to replace Boudreau in the field, which led to trade discussions by Veeck. But the media got wind of it, and the Cleveland News launched a "Boudreau Ballot," giving fans the opportunity to vote to keep or trade Boudreau the shortstop. The result was overwhelmingly in favor of keeping Boudreau, not trading him—and, thus, making it unnecessary to replace him as manager.

Veeck had no choice and, consequently, the Indians went on to win the pennant in 1948 with Boudreau as their manager and, of course, their shortstop. But it wasn't easy. The Indians were involved in a four-team race most of the season and reached the final day tied with Boston, each with 96–58 records. It was partially achieved because of an August doubleheader against New York, which the Indians swept, with Boudreau in the starring role.

Boudreau hadn't played all week as he was nursing several injuries, nor was he expected to play that day. But late in the first game, the Indians loaded the bases with the score tied and two outs, and Boudreau made a dramatic appearance as a pinch hitter.

He strapped on a shoe over his heavily taped left foot, limped to the plate, and delivered a two-run single that eventually decided the game. The Indians went on to win the nightcap as well, and Veeck called Boudreau's hit "the most dramatic thing I've ever seen in baseball."

Then, in the climactic playoff game after the Indians and Red Sox finished in a tie, Boudreau hammered two homers and two singles to lead the Indians to an 8–3 victory and the pennant. They went on to beat the Boston Braves in the World Series.

Veeck was ecstatic. "We didn't win the pennant in 1948," he said. "We won it on November 24, 1947, the day I rehired Boudreau [as manager]."

Boudreau's career in Cleveland ended in 1950 after Veeck sold the team. But the "Boy Manager," who died in 2001 at age 84, will long be remembered, especially by the fans of the Boudreau era. As Franklin Lewis wrote in the Cleveland Press: "What Veeck didn't know before he decided to stick with Boudreau—but learned afterward—was that, in Cleveland, Lou Boudreau [was] immortal."

Make that immortal and remarkable, as stated so eloquently by Kuhn.

Year	Tm	G	AB	R	H	HR	RBI	SB	BB	SO	BA
1938–1950	CLE (13 yrs)	1560	5754	823	1706	63	740	50	766	297	.296
1951–1952	BOS (2 yrs)	86	275	38	73	5	49	1	30	12	.265
Total		1646	6029	861	1779	68	789	51	796	309	.295

Wesley Ferrell

Wesley Ferrell was another of those "coulda," "shoulda," "woulda" players who could have, should have, and probably would have had a Hall of Fame career if he'd had better control of his temper.

Too often it seemed that Ferrell's competitive fire failed him, actually worked against him, causing him—and his team—more pain than gain. During Ferrell's seven years with the Indians, which began when he was only 19 in 1927, he was suspended three times for temper tantrums. Once, in 1932 when Roger Peckinpaugh managed the Indians, Ferrell was fined $1,500 and suspended for ten days for refusing to leave a game when he was replaced by a reliever.

Unfortunately for Ferrell his hot temper was a factor that led to his being traded in the wake of an 11–12 season in 1933 to the Red Sox on May 25, 1934. The deal came in the wake of a third contract holdout by Ferrell (whose top salary was $20,000 in 1931, the year after he'd gone 25–13 for the Indians).

There still are many who believe that his 193 career victories (with 128 losses) and a no-hitter (April 29, 1931, 9–0, vs. St. Louis Browns) are—or should be—enough for him to be voted into the Hall of Fame by the Veterans Committee.

His supporters always cite the fact that he won more games than four starting pitchers already in the Hall of Fame: Lefty Gomez (189), Sandy Koufax (165), Addie Joss (160), and Dizzy Dean (150). Rube Waddell, another Hall of Famer, also won 193 games.

It's the same argument stressed by supporters of Mel Harder, who have been trying for years, without success, to get him elected. Harder's lifetime record is 223–186.

With his trade to the Red Sox in 1934 providing the "change in scenery" argument as being all that Ferrell needed, he rebounded with a 14–5

won-lost record. Ferrell was even better in 1935 when he was the American League's winningest pitcher with a 25–14 record. That was the year Ferrell pitched 42 games, started 38, and completed 31.

In 1936, Ferrell was 20–15, the sixth time in eight seasons that he won 20 or more games, although his record went downhill thereafter—and it probably was not coincidental that his temperament continued to blaze as fiercely as ever.

It was in 1937 that Ferrell got himself in trouble with Red Sox manager (and future AL president and Hall of Famer) Joe Cronin and was fined $1,000 for walking off the mound without having been replaced by another pitcher. That incident led to Ferrell being traded on July 11, 1937, to Washington, and he wound up his major league career with three other teams—New York Yankees, Brooklyn, and Boston Braves—from 1938 to 1941.

But Ferrell was not finished with baseball—and neither was the competitive fire within him extinguished. In fact, it nearly got him suspended for life from Organized Baseball.

Ferrell returned to the minor leagues as a manager-pitcher in 1942. On one occasion he became so irate by what he considered an incorrect decision that he not only punched the umpire but also took his team off the field.

It is interesting to note that one of Ferrell's idiosyncrasies was that he reportedly often walked around golf courses looking for bees because he had a firm belief that getting stung on his arm made him a better pitcher. Maybe so.

However, the belief among many of his supporters is that he could have, should have, and probably would have been an even more successful pitcher—and in the Hall of Fame today—if only he'd controlled his temper as well as he did his pitches.

Year	Tm	W	L	ERA	GS	CG	SHO	IP	H	R	BB	SO
1927–1933	CLE (7 yrs)	102	62	3.67	157	113	8	1321	1373	644	526	516
1934–1936	BOS (4 yrs)	62	40	4.11	110	81	9	877	982	462	310	314
1937–1938	WSH (2 yrs)	24	21	4.77	46	30	0	356	407	222	156	128
1938–1939	NYY (2 yrs)	3	4	6.75	7	2	0	49	66	43	35	13
1940	BRO (1 yr)	0	0	6.75	0	0	0	4	4	3	4	4
1941	BSN (1 yr)	2	1	5.14	3	1	0	14	13	8	9	10
Total		193	128	4.04	323	227	17	2623	2845	1382	1040	985

Hal Trosky

A severe case of migraine headaches cost Hal Trosky what would have been an outstanding baseball career. It also deprived the Indians of a player who was—and probably would have continued to be—one of their all-time best power hitters. The mysterious ailment, still not completely understood, struck Trosky at the height of his career as the Tribe's long-sought, home-run-hitting first baseman in the late 1930s and into the 1940s.

After he batted .295 with 25 homers and 93 RBI in 1940, Trosky played only part-time the following season and then retired. But his retirement turned out to be only temporary—apparently only until he got away from the Indians—or gained relief from the migraine headaches that plagued him earlier.

He returned to play in 1944 at age 31 but, again, not for long. What's more—he returned to the game with the White Sox after requesting the Indians deal him to the Chicago club, which was closer to his farm in Norway, Iowa. He proceeded to play two more seasons, though not consecutively nor with the ability he'd possessed earlier.

Trosky batted .241 with 10 homers and 40 RBI for the White Sox in 135 games in 1944 but sat out the season in 1945, reportedly for a recurrence of the migraine headaches. He returned again in 1946 but played only 88 games, hit .254 with two homers and 31 RBI, and retired again, this time for good.

The record book shows that Trosky was something extra special for the Indians earlier, from 1933, when he joined them as a 20-year-old rookie, through 1941. This was the case especially in 1936 when Trosky's .343 average included 42 homers and featured 162 RBI, the most in the American League.

He drove in more than 100 runs in six consecutive seasons (1934–39) and batted .300 or better four times. It also was in 1936 that Trosky put together a 28-game hitting streak and was compared to future Hall of Famer Lou Gehrig. On two occasions Trosky hammered three homers in a game: the first on May 12, 1934, against Chicago, and again on July 3, 1947 against the St. Louis Browns.

Trosky was especially prolific when the Indians played at League Park, which was then their home field until 1946. With its short right field fence (290 feet from the plate and 40 feet high), League Park was ideal for a left-handed power hitter like Trosky, who died in 1979 at age 66.

In addition to his migraine headaches, it also has been speculated that Trosky's problems were attributed to the Indians' failure to win the pennant in 1940. According to a 1949 book about the Indians, authored by Franklin Lewis, former sports editor of the *Cleveland Press,* Trosky was the ringleader of the team's rebellion against manager Oscar Vitt. The Indians lost the pennant to Detroit by one game that season.

The allegation tarnished the reputation of Trosky, one of the Tribe's senior leaders, but it was denied by several members of the "revolt," including Trosky. As pointed out later by Mel Harder, another senior member of the 1940 team, "Trosky didn't even attend the meeting we had with Bradley . . . he had gone home because his mother had died."

We may never know whether Trosky's premature retirement from the Indians was caused by his uneasiness at being wrongly identified as the leader of the attempt to oust Vitt or by the extreme severity of his migraine headaches. Perhaps it was a combination of both. Whatever the cause, it cost the Indians a player who might have become one of their greatest.

Year	Tm	G	AB	R	H	HR	RBI	SB	BB	SO	BA
1933–1941	CLE (9 yrs)	1124	4365	758	1365	216	911	21	449	373	.313
1944–1946	CHW (2 yrs)	223	796	77	196	12	101	7	96	67	.246
Total		1347	5161	835	1561	228	1012	28	545	440	.302

Ken Keltner

You won't find the answer in the record book, and most stories would start with something about Joe DiMaggio or the New York Yankees.

However, if it were possible to ask the players in the game that night—July 17, 1941—or, even any of the 67,468 fans in Cleveland Municipal Stadium to see the Indians play the Yankees, their opinions of what transpired would vary.

DiMaggio would say that because it rained that day the ground was wet, making it difficult to run the bases. Roger Peckinpaugh, then the Indians manager, would give credit to his pitchers, Al Smith and Jim Bagby Jr. And Lefty Gomez, DiMaggio's roommate, would blame the first base umpire, Bill Summers. But Harry Jones, the baseball writer covering the Indians for the *Plain Dealer,* and the official scorer would say it was Ken Keltner. "I didn't call it . . . the umpire did," he said.

That is, it was Keltner who deserves most of the credit for the Indians stopping DiMaggio's record 56-game hitting streak. DiMaggio went 0 for 4, grounding out three times, and each time slipping on the wet path between home and first base.

Smith and Bagby combined on a six-hitter, though the Indians lost 4–3.

Gomez lamented the call by Summers, the first base umpire, on the groundout retiring DiMaggio by half a step in the first inning.

And in his final at bat in the eighth inning, DiMaggio grounded into a 6–4–3 double play—Lou Boudreau to Ray Mack to Oscar Grimes.

When it was over, Keltner was noncommittal. "Joe was right, it was hard to run because the ground was still wet . . . and Smitty and Bags pitched great, it's too bad one had to lose. I couldn't see if my throw beat Joe or not. But if Summers said he was out, he was out."

The bottom line is that we lost. The big thing wasn't stopping Joe, it was we didn't win the game," said Keltner.

His two plays on DiMaggio were textbook examples of how to play third base. Keltner was playing very deep and close to the foul line for both. "Knowing Joe, I knew he wouldn't bunt," Keltner said. "And because the ground was so soggy he would have trouble getting out of the batter's box. I just played him deep and waited for him to hit the ball to me."

DiMaggio did, and each time Keltner fired laser-shot throws to Grimes at first base. As for Jones, "All I did was write down 5–3—Keltner to Grimes," he said. "I didn't make the call [on DiMaggio in the first inning], Summers did." And so ended DiMaggio's hitting streak—a record that was set eight decades ago, one that still stands.

More important to Keltner than making the best plays of the game to blank DiMaggio, he said, "OK, they were good. But I would've rather won the game."

Then, was it the most memorable game in Keltner's career? He began with the Indians in 1938 and continued for 11 seasons through 1949, during which he delivered 163 home runs.

He shrugged and said, "The most memorable game, the one I'll never forget, was the playoff [against Boston] in 1948 when we and the Red Sox finished [the regular season] in a tie," and forcing a one-game playoff.

The Indians won, 8–3, with Keltner once again playing a key role. In the fourth inning, he batted against Denny Galehouse with two runners aboard and the game tied, 1–1, and he hammered a homer. The Indians won, 8–3. "How could any game compare to that one?" he asked.

None could. Not even the game that stopped DiMaggio's record-hitting streak—a record that might never be broken.

Year	Tm	G	AB	R	H	HR	RBI	SB	BB	SO	BA
1937–1949	CLE (12 yrs)	1513	5655	735	1561	163	850	39	511	474	.276
1950	BOS (1 yr)	13	28	2	9	0	2	0	3	6	.321
Total		1526	5683	737	1570	163	852	39	514	480	.276

Jeff Heath

The accolades came fast—*too fast,* as it turned out—for Jeff Heath, whose career with the Indians blazed brightly at the beginning but soon flamed out.

Oscar Vitt, the once highly respected manager of the Indians whose career eventually took a nosedive, was the first to heap praise on Heath. In his first spring training as the Tribe manager in 1938, Vitt marveled at the presumed ability of Heath, then a rookie getting his first trial with the Tribe. After Vitt watched Heath take batting practice, the manager gushed lavish praise for the Canadian-born outfielder, calling him "the best natural hitter I've seen since Joe Jackson."

Initially Heath did resemble Jackson, coming within .006 of winning the American League batting championship in 1938. Jimmie Foxx finished first with a .349 average, and Heath was second at .343, an average that included 21 homers and 112 RBI.

Heath never hit that well again during his 14-year major league career, though he came close several times during his eight-plus seasons with the Indians through 1945. However, after that initial season, Heath's average dropped to .292 in 1939 and fell even further to .219 in 1940.

That's the year the Indians were in total turmoil—and mockingly nicknamed "Cleveland Cry Babies"—because they staged a rebellion against Vitt. He was replaced in 1941 by Roger Peckinpaugh, who also immediately fell in love with Heath's batting prowess.

And, again, Heath delivered. He batted .340 with 24 homers and 123 RBI in 1941. It was the second of six times that he hit .300, and he quickly regained his stature as a fan favorite, if not a favorite of the media covering the team.

Heath was very sensitive to criticism and in 1940, when he was among the players who met with Indians owner Alva Bradley in the so-called "Vitt Rebellion," he became very angry at Ed McAuley of the *Cleveland News.* McAuley suggested that Heath ought to be a better team player and that he should give 100 percent effort all the time. Heath responded by threatening to throw McAuley out of the clubhouse if he ever showed up again. McAuley did, the very next day, but instead of being physically abused by Heath, the player greeted McAuley with a big grin and handshake and, ostensibly, all was forgiven.

It later came out that, after Heath's threat was reported, Bradley sent a message that was posted in the clubhouse. It stated: "Tell Heath that if he touches one hair on McAuley's head I will see to it that he never plays one more inning in Organized Baseball."

Obviously, Bradley's warning cooled Heath's wrath, and Heath even went on to comply with McAuley's suggestion of being a better team player and giving 100 percent effort all the time.

Heath ended up hitting .300 in six of his 14 seasons in the major leagues and finished his career with Washington, the St. Louis Browns, and Boston Braves from 1946 to 1949. He died in 1975 at age 60.

Heath was one of the leaders with the Braves in 1948, when he batted .319 with 20 homers and 76 RBI—and eagerly awaited an opportunity to beat his former team, the Indians, in the World Series. But he couldn't because, in one of the Braves' final games, less than a week prior to the start of the Series, Heath slid into home and suffered a broken ankle.

It all but ended his career as he played in only 36 games for the Braves in 1949. The man who, 11 years earlier, had been called "the best natural hitter since Joe Jackson" was finished.

Year	Tm	G	AB	R	H	HR	RBI	SB	BB	SO	BA
1936–1945	CLE (10 yrs)	957	3489	546	1040	122	619	52	366	438	.298
1946	WSH (1 yr)	48	166	23	47	4	27	0	36	36	.283
1946–1947	SLB (2 yrs)	227	807	127	210	39	142	2	125	124	.260
1948–1949	BSN (2 yrs)	151	475	81	150	29	99	2	66	72	.316
Total		1383	4937	777	1447	194	887	56	593	670	.293

Joe Vosmik

Joe Vosmik played for the Indians in the 1930s when a box seat at League Park cost $3.50, and nobody ever heard of a player's agent, let alone used one.

Two anecdotes survive Vosmik in yellowed newspaper accounts. One tells how Vosmik, who grew up on Cleveland's East Side, got his start in professional baseball because he was a "good looking blond-haired kid who looks like a Viking and plays hard." The other tells about a decision Vosmik made in the 1935 season of his seven-year career with the Indians (and 13 in the major leagues) that he lived to regret.

First, the "Viking" story.

Vosmik was playing on an amateur team and Billy Evans, then general manager of the Indians, and his wife were out to dinner when he suggested they stop to see an all-star sandlot game. "I don't think there's anybody we'd be interested in, but I should make an appearance," Evans told his wife.

Afterward she asked Evans if he'd seen anybody who looked good. He said no, then asked her—with mocking sincerity—"did anybody look good to you?"

As reported in the newspaper back then, Mrs. Evans replied, "I don't know much about baseball, but that good-looking blond-haired kid who looks like a Viking sure plays hard. Why don't you give him a tryout?"

The next day Evans met the parents of the "good-looking blond-haired kid who looked like a Viking." It was Vosmik, and he jumped at Evans's offer, though it really wasn't an offer, only a tryout with the Indians.

Vosmik passed the trial and three years later, after two good seasons in the minor leagues, he was wearing an Indians' uniform, which he did from 1931 to 1937. In those seven years he batted .300 four times, including .348 in 1935.

Vosmik ended his career in 1944 after playing with the St. Louis Browns, Boston Braves, Brooklyn, and Washington, and batted .300 two more times for a total of six. He died in 1962 at age 51.

It was Vosmik's .348 batting average in 1935 that comes into play in the second part of this story. He went into the final day of that season in a doubleheader against St. Louis, leading the American League by three percentage points over Buddy Myer of Washington.

Because the Indians were solidly lodged in third place, Vosmik asked manager Steve O'Neill if he could sit out the first game to protect his .348 average. However, he did pinch hit in the ninth inning of the opener and made an out. But Myer would still need to gain three points.

Then, between games, Vosmik was told that Myer had gone 4 for 5 against Philadelphia in Washington's final game, raising his average four points, one ahead of Vosmik. Thus, Vosmik needed to play the second game of the Tribe's doubleheader and get at least two hits to regain the lead. Vosmik singled in his first at bat but then was retired twice through six innings, leaving his average one point behind Myer. However, before Vosmik could bat again, the game was called because of darkness. As a result, Myer finished with a .349026 average (215-for-616) and Vosmik's final mark was .348387 (216 for 620), meaning Vosmik lost the batting championships by .000639. One more hit—which he might have made if he'd played the first game, or if the second game had not been called early—would have given Vosmik a .350 average and the batting crown.

It was unfortunate because Vosmik was a longtime fan favorite—for which he had Mrs. Billy Evans to thank, even though she was the first to admit she knew nothing about baseball.

Year	Tm	G	AB	R	H	HR	RBI	SB	BB	SO	BA
1930–1936	CLE (7 yrs)	824	3207	480	1003	44	556	17	312	147	.313
1937	SLB (1 yr)	144	594	81	193	4	93	2	49	38	.325
1938–1939	BOS (2 yrs)	291	1175	210	354	16	170	4	125	59	.301
1940–1941	BRO (2 yrs)	141	460	45	125	1	46	0	26	25	.272
1944	WSH (1 yr)	14	36	2	7	0	9	0	2	3	.194
Total		1414	5472	818	1682	65	874	23	514	272	.307

Willis Hudlin

Sixty-five years after the fact, Willis Hudlin could still see the ball soaring over the right-field fence at League Park and remembered exactly how he felt. "I felt like hell," said the former workhorse of the Indians pitching staff who was a mainstay on the team for 14-plus seasons, from 1926 when he was 20, and continuing through 475 games when he was "liberated, thankfully" in 1940.

Hudlin said he "felt like hell" because the home run he allowed 65 years earlier on August 11, 1929, was the 500th of Babe Ruth's career. "Everybody knew [Ruth] was getting close, but nobody wanted to be the guy who gave up the big one," said Hudlin.

In those days Hudlin never gained the renown that others on the Indians pitching staff did, but according to some of those "others," he certainly deserved more credit than he usually received.

A quiet and unassuming man, Hudlin seldom spoke in headlines or was highly publicized; nor did he have a well-known name or even a well-known pitching record. But he was the "backbone" of what was then the Tribe pitching staff throughout the 1930s, according to Mel Harder.

It's the reason he was called "Ace" by Harder, as well as Wes Ferrell and even Bob Feller. "Ace was always there to help one of us, physically and emotionally," said Harder in an interview in 2002, when Hudlin died at age 86, a few months before Harder also passed on. "We were very good friends, during and after our careers ended," added Harder. "I think it is fair to say that the rest of us, myself included, got most of the headlines back then, but we considered Hudlin our leader, the ace of the staff."

Whether he got his share of credit or not, and despite the fact that among his 157–151 won-lost record in 14-plus seasons with the Indians, Hudlin never won 20 games. He came close in his first full season in Cleveland in 1927, when his record was 18–12, and again in

1929, when it was 17–15. Those were the years Hudlin became known in the media as a "Yankee Killer" because he beat New York 11 times in those three seasons.

And last but not least among Hudlin's underpublicized pitching credits is that he is still the seventh winningest pitcher in Tribe history. Those who won more games for Cleveland were Feller (266), Harder (223), Bob Lemon (207), Stan Coveleski (172), Early Wynn (164), and Addie Joss (160)—and all but Harder are in the Hall of Fame.

Despite the only "blemish" on his career—though it's probably unfair to consider it as such—establishing Ruth as the first player to reach the 500 mark in homers, he went on to hit 714 for a record, since surpassed by Barry Bonds's 762 in 2007.

It doesn't mean much now, especially with so many players in the "600 Club" (i.e., 600 career home runs), but back then, in 1929, it was a big thing—take it from Hudlin. "It was a sinker, my best pitch, but that time it didn't sink—or at least it didn't sink enough," said Hudlin in a 1994 interview.

"I can still see it flying over that damned right field fence [290 feet away from home plate]," Hudlin recalled.

As for that "liberated, thankfully" remark by Hudlin, it pertained to the infamous Indians rebellion of 1940, when a group of players petitioned owner Alva Bradley to replace manager Oscar Vitt. Hudlin was not one of the players in the meeting expressing their displeasure with Vitt, though he was in agreement in spirit with them.

"Actually, I was liberated, thankfully, a couple of weeks earlier than the guys went in to see Mr. Bradley," said Hudlin. "I was 2–1 at the time and [Vitt] was no happier with me than I was with him, so it was an even trade-off."

Hudlin went on to pitch for the St. Louis Browns, Washington, and the New York Giants through 1944 and retired.

Year	Tm	W	L	ERA	GS	CG	SHO	IP	H	R	BB	SO
1926–1940	CLE (15 yrs)	157	151	4.34	320	154	11	2557	2930	1436	832	662
1940, 1944	SLB (2 yrs)	0	2	10.13	1	0	0	13	22	18	8	5
1940	WSH (1 yr)	1	2	6.51	6	1	0	37	50	33	5	9
1940	NYG (1 yr)	0	1	10.80	1	0	0	5	9	6	1	1
Total		158	156	4.41	328	155	11	2613	3011	1493	846	677

1951–1975

Bob Lemon

It was 1946 and Bob Lemon, fresh out of the Navy, was reporting to his first Indians spring training camp as a highly touted third baseman. He would compete with veteran Ken Keltner who was attempting a comeback at age 30.

But after several weeks, Lemon did not make a promising impression on manager Lou Boudreau. He didn't hit as the Indians had hoped or as Lemon had expected.

Because Lemon had good hands and a great arm, Boudreau decided to try him in center field. Thus, Lemon was the Tribe's center fielder on Opening Day and played well enough—even made a spectacular diving catch to preserve Bob Feller's 1–0 victory over Chicago—though his bat remained quiet. It did, so through Lemon's first 55 games as he hit only .180 and Boudreau was looking for help.

Then, one day something happened during a routine game of catch between Lemon and Mel Harder. "We were playing the Yankees and before the game, Lem and I were warming up in front of the dugout," said Harder. "Lem threw me a ball that moved so much I almost missed it. When I yelled something to him, Bill Dickey came over and laughed with me."

Dickey was a veteran catcher for the Yankees who, like Harder, was winding up his playing career. "[Dickey] had been in the Navy with Lem and caught him when [Lemon] was pitching in pickup games. He suggested we ought to think of possibly making Lemon a pitcher."

They did, and it proved to be a turning point for Lemon.

In that 1946 season Lemon went on to make 32 appearances on the mound, five as a starter. Though he won only four games and lost five, his earned run average was 2.49 and the die was cast.

In the next 13 seasons through 1958, Lemon fashioned a Hall of Fame career. "He had a natural sinker and once he learned that he didn't have to throw as hard as he could, Lem became a good pitcher," said Harder.

Lemon was a 20-game winner seven times, led AL pitchers in victories four times, won a career total of 207 games, was on the all-star team seven times, pitched a no-hitter and two one-hitters, and even saved 22 games as a sometimes reliever. He also won two games in the 1948 World Series when the Indians beat the Boston Braves.

Lemon was elected the Indians Man of the Year in 1949, and he shared the award with two of his pitching teammates, Early Wynn and Mike Garcia, in 1952.

After leaving the Indians, he held several scouting and managerial jobs the next eight years and won the minor league Manager of the Year award after piloting Seattle in the Pacific Coast League in 1966. That's when, in 1967, he applied for the Indians managerial job but was rejected by Gabe Paul. Later—in fact on the day Lemon was inducted into the Hall of Fame in 1976—Paul called his rejection of Lemon the biggest mistake he made in baseball.

Lemon, who died in 2000 at age 79, managed the Kansas City Royals, Chicago White Sox, and New York Yankees. He took the Yankees to the World Series in 1981, after which George Steinbrenner, the late owner of the Yankees, rewarded Lemon with a lifetime contract.

It could be considered the culmination of a true miracle that began in 1946, which Lemon himself was among the first to admit. As he said one day when he was in Cleveland with the Yankees, "Maybe it's a good thing I was so lousy a hitter. Otherwise I might have spent my life working—instead of playing [baseball]."

Which was true. Very true.

Year	Tm	W	L	ERA	GS	CG	SHO	IP	H	R	BB	SO
1946–1958	CLE (13 yrs)	207	128	3.23	350	188	31	2850	2559	1185	1251	1277

Early Wynn

Early Wynn pitched 691 games during his 23-year Hall of Fame career and probably remembered every one that he played for three teams, including the Indians from 1949 to 1957 and again in 1963.

"Aw, don't make me out to be something I'm not," Wynn grumbled one night after his baseball career ended and he was broadcasting for the Toronto Blue Jays. "I was a pitcher, a pretty *good* pitcher, but I was just a guy who worked hard to get to the big leagues and worked hard to stay in the big leagues. That's it," said Wynn who died in 1999 at age 79.

But there's something else he was . . . a fraud.

Wynn cultivated a reputation for being gruff and tough when he was on the mound winning 300 games—and especially when he was on the mound *losing* 244 games.

All of which led to the question: was there one game that he remembered best of all? "There wasn't just one, there were two," he said. "One was the third game I pitched and lost, 1–0 [when he was 19 years old], and the other was the last game I pitched and won [when he was 43].

"The first was in Yankee Stadium in 1939. I was with Washington then. I was getting past guys like DiMaggio, Keller, Gordon, and Henrich, and that little pip-squeak shortstop got me," said Wynn. He meant Phil Rizzuto. "[Rizzuto] hit a ball one inch around the foul pole in left field for a game-winner. It was the only run of the game.

I should have got him, drilled him, the next time he came up, but I was new in the league and so was he. I never let anything like that happen again," he said.

And what about the other game he'd never forget? "That was my 300th [victory in 1963]. It was in Kansas City and was the fifth time I tried to get it,"

said Wynn. "I went into that game thinking about Rizzuto, believe it or not," he said. "I kept thinking, 'If I had not let that little pip-squeak hit that game-winning homer we probably would have won and I wouldn't have to pitch five games now to win 300.'"

Three hundred victories literally guarantee election to the Hall of Fame, to which Wynn was inducted in 1972. In that game on July 13, 1963, Wynn and the Indians were leading 5–4, through five innings, and he turned the game over to his roommate, Jerry Walker, who hung on to save it, 7–4.

Wynn came from Washington in 1949 in one of the Indians' best-ever trades: he and first baseman Mickey Vernon for first baseman Eddie Robinson and pitchers Joe Haynes and Ed Klieman.

And then, ironically, he was virtually given away in 1957 by Frank Lane in one of the team's worst-ever deals: he and outfielder Al Smith were traded to the Chicago White Sox for infielder Fred Hatfield and outfielder Minnie Minoso.

The White Sox released Wynn after the 1962 season and the Tribe signed him to give him a chance to win his 300th game.

Between that first loss and last victory, Wynn won 20 games five times, including 23 with the Indians in 1954 and 22 with the White Sox in 1959 when he was the American League's winningest pitcher. That also was the year he won the AL Cy Young Award.

And while he was—and *wanted* to be—known as a cantankerous, ornery, curmudgeon and cultivated the reputation by claiming he'd knock down his own grandmother if she crowded the plate, those who knew Early Wynn knew him as one of the game's "good guys"—and a fraud.

Year	Tm	W	L	ERA	GS	CG	SHO	IP	H	R	BB	SO
1949–57, 63	CLE(10 yrs)	164	102	3.24	296	144	24	2286	2037	923	877	1277
1939–1948	WSH (8 yrs)	72	87	3.94	168	92	9	1266	1359	655	460	386
1958–1962	CHW (5 yrs)	64	55	3.72	148	54	16	1010	895	459	438	671
Total		300	244	3.54	612	290	49	4564	4291	2037	1775	2334

Mike Garcia

It was Leo Durocher who once suggested that nice guys finish last, promoting the theory that it was necessary to be mean and tough to play on a winning team. Among those who would have proved him wrong was Mike Garcia, a member of the Tribe's vaunted "Big Four," although it could have been called the "Big Five" when the Indians set a record by winning 111 games in 1954.

Along with Garcia (19–8), probably the most underrated pitcher of the five, the staff also included Bob Feller (13–3), Bob Lemon (23–7), Early Wynn (23–11), and Art Houtteman (15–7). Garcia led the AL with a 2.64 ERA that year, and his won-lost record was something of a misnomer. His victory total easily could have been at least 20 or more.

Here's how Garcia got tagged as a "nice guy," which he was, on and off the field.

Late in the 1954 season it was apparent that the Indians were going to win the pennant—the only question being whether they would win enough games to break the AL won-lost record of 110–44 set by the New York Yankees in 1927.

As Garcia explained it prior to his death in 1986 at age 62: "Al Lopez [then the Indians manager] said he wanted to go for the record and asked if I'd be willing to pitch out of the bull pen.

I'd already won 19 and wanted to go for 20 and, as I told Lopez, the difference between winning 19 and 20 is like the difference between a Ford and a Cadillac. But I also told him I'd do it if that's what he wanted, and Lopez said, 'I'll see to it that you pickup at least another victory, don't worry.'

When we got down to the final game, I sill hadn't won one more, so Lopez started me against Detroit. But he also put all the scrub-beenies in the lineup, not the regular guys who carried us to the record all season."

As it turned out, the tenacious "Big Bear" and the scrub-beenies battled the Tigers for 12 innings before he left with a 6–6 tie. Then Detroit scored twice in the 13th and won against reliever Ray Narleski. Despite all that happened, it was a good season for Garcia. On May 16 he threw a one-hitter against Philadelphia.

He also was very good in 1951 (20–13), 1952 (22–11), and 1953 (18–9), and was a member of the AL all-star team in 1952, 1953, and 1954. Unfortunately for Garcia—and the Indians—he ran into physical problems after the 1954 season, and his career careened downhill.

In 1958 he slipped on a wet mound and suffered a slipped disc in his back that prevented him from pitching after only six starts. Then, after undergoing back surgery, Garcia re-signed with the Indians and attempted a comeback in 1959, but he couldn't duplicate the success he'd previously enjoyed.

Garcia played with the Chicago White Sox in 1959 but then suffered another setback in a freak accident while working on a racing car that he operated as a hobby. The Big Bear lost the tip of his right index finger and, while he recovered in time to pitch 15 games as a reliever for the White Sox, his career was soon over. He pitched for Chicago in 1960 without a decision and was released.

He tried again with Washington and, in 16 games in 1961, also in relief, was 0–1 and retired with a 147–97 career won-lost record.

And thus, the bottom line for the Big Bear: he was a good guy who, contrary to what Leo Durocher always preached, was a winner—although, his winning ended too soon.

Year	Tm	W	L	ERA	GS	CG	SHO	IP	H	R	BB	SO
1948–1959	CLE (12 yrs)	142	96	3.24	281	111	27	2138	2102	865	696	1095
1960	CHW (1 yr)	0	0	4.58	0	0	0	17	23	9	10	8
1961	WSA (1 yr)	0	1	4.74	0	0	0	19	23	14	13	14
Total		142	97	3.27	281	111	27	2174	2148	888	719	1117

Al Rosen

Al Rosen chuckled as he answered the question, but there's no doubt it still rankles him even though it happened more than half a century ago. "I'm asked that question a lot of times so I am used to dealing with it, and besides, what else can I do about it now," said Rosen.

It happened in 1953 when Rosen was a 29-year-old third baseman for the Indians. It's when he lost the Triple Crown, one of baseball's most coveted hitting honors by .00006 percentage point.

Rosen won the American League's Most Valuable Player award, as well as the RBI (145) and home run (43) championships that season—but not the Triple Crown. He batted *only* .335559, rounded to .336, to Washington's Mickey Vernon's .337171, rounded to a league-leading .337.

Going into that final game, Rosen was hitting an even .333, while Vernon's average was .335. When Rosen got two hits in his first four at bats, it gave him a .337 mark and what appeared to be the lead by a fraction of one point over Vernon.

But then came word that Vernon also went 2 for 4 in Washington's final game, meaning Rosen needed another hit in his last at bat (for a .338 average) to retain the lead. It didn't happen. And, to make it even more agonizing, Rosen was retired on a "bang-bang" play at first base as he grounded to the third baseman whose throw beat him at first base by "half a step."

The quotation marks around that half a step belong to Rosen—though not to Indians manager Al Lopez and most of the Cleveland players.

And, until the day he died in 2005, Lopez swore the umpire "blew" the call. "Rosie beat the throw and should have had a hit," Lopez insisted. However, Rosen, always a gentleman as a player and later as chief executive of three other major league teams (New York Yankees, Houston Astros, and San Francisco Giants), refused to second-guess the umpire's decision, even five decades later. "I think he called it right," said Rosen. "Maybe if I hadn't jumped at the [first base] bag with my last step I might have beaten the throw . . . but I am not even sure about that," he said.

That 1953 season was Rosen's best of seven good years with the Indians. He wore a Cleveland uniform for ten seasons, from the final weeks in 1947 through 1956, but he wasn't in the lineup regularly from 1947 to 1949.

He also led the AL with 37 homers in 1950, and was the RBI leader with 105 in 1952, which was one of five consecutive seasons he drove in more than 100 runs. He retired in 1956 at 32 with a career batting average of .285 and 192 homers and 717 RBI.

If he has any regrets, they are primarily about what happened to the Indians in 1954, when they set a major league record with 111 victories but then were swept in the World Series by the New York Giants. "I am still convinced we were the better team," said Rosen.

So why did the Tribe get blown out by the Giants? "I don't know," said Rosen. "There are a lot of theories, beginning with the longtime favorite that we were worn out because we were more interested in setting a record for winning the most games. But I never bought that. It was just one of those things. That's baseball. That's life. Who can explain it? Why even try? All I am saying is that we were the best. We should have won. But we didn't."

The same probably could be said about Rosen's failed—no, make that *unsuccessful*—effort to win the Triple Crown in 1953.

Year	Tm	G	AB	R	H	HR	RBI	SB	BB	SO	BA
1947–1956	(CLE 10 Yrs)	1044	3725	603	1063	192	717	39	587	385	.285

Larry Doby

This was 1947, shortly after Larry Doby was signed by the Indians on July 2, as the second African American player to break baseball's color barrier, as Jackie Robinson had done 11 weeks earlier.

In one of Doby's early games, he lashed a single to right center field, rounded first, and sprinted for second. But the outfielder's throw beat Doby, and the shortstop slapped a tag on him. As Doby was getting to his feet, the shortstop spit tobacco juice in his face, sneered and said, "Welcome to the big leagues."

Doby recalled the incident prior to his 1998 induction into the Hall of Fame. He died in 2003 at age 79. "I was angry. I wanted to hit him, but I knew I couldn't do anything," said Doby, "because it would have made it even more difficult, maybe ruined it for me and anybody who followed me and Jackie. All I could do was wipe his spit off my face and walk away."

That's the way it was for Doby, as it was, obviously, for Robinson. However, several of Doby's former teammates believe that his introduction as the American League's first African American player was even more difficult than Robinson's. As one said, "Jackie was better prepared. Branch Rickey looked a long time for the right guy, and then he coached Jackie, warned him as to what he'd be facing."

It also was difficult for Bill Veeck, who was quoted as saying that, after signing Doby, he received an estimated 20,000 pieces of hate mail. Later, in 1948, it got better, when Doby was a major force in Cleveland winning the pennant and World Series.

Doby also was a leader in 1954 when the Indians won another pennant and his 126 RBI and 32 homers were the best in the AL. Doby also led the league with 32 homers in 1955 and made the all-star team six times.

Following his ninth season in Cleveland, Doby was involved in a series of trades. After batting .291 in 1955, the Indians dealt him to the Chicago White Sox. Then he was traded to Baltimore in December 1957, to Cleveland in 1958, to Detroit in March 1959, and two months later back to the White Sox. Shortly thereafter Doby retired as an active player.

He scouted and coached for several teams, and he returned again to Cleveland in 1973, this time as a coach under Ken Aspromonte, during which it appeared he would become a trailblazer again—as baseball's first African American manager.

Doby was the choice of Indians president Ted Bonda to replace Aspromonte. But, reportedly unknown to Bonda, general manager Phil Seghi preferred Frank Robinson, whom he'd known from the time both were previously with the Cincinnati Reds.

Thus, Seghi claimed Robinson on waivers as a player in September of 1974 and less than a month later hired him to be the Indians player-manager in 1975.

And when Aspromonte was fired and replaced by Robinson, Doby—despite being the choice of Bonda—was out. However, it didn't end Doby's uniformed career in baseball. Still in the picture was Veeck, owner of the White Sox, and in 1978 he hired Doby to manage his team. Thus, once again, Doby became the *second* African American to break baseball's color line, this time as a manager.

But the White Sox under Doby were very bad, and he was replaced. And so ended the uniformed baseball career of Larry Doby.

A trailblazer from beginning to end. Or, if you will, a *near* trailblazer from beginning to end.

Year	Tm	G	AB	R	H	HR	RBI	SB	BB	SO	BA
1947–55, 58	CLE (10 yrs)	1235	4315	808	1234	215	776	44	703	805	.286
1956–57, 59	CHW (3 yrs)	280	978	147	269	38	190	3	160	197	.275
1959	DET (1 yr)	18	55	5	12	0	4	0	8	9	.218
Total		1533	5348	960	1515	253	970	47	871	1011	.283

Rocky Colavito

Of the 1,841 games Rocky Colavito played in a 14-year major league baseball career, two stand out as "unforgettable," one as a highlight, the other as a "lowlight."

The first happened June 10, 1959, against the Orioles in Baltimore. Colavito entered the record book with "baseball's greatest single accomplishment," as the *Sporting News* called it: four home runs in one game. It's a record Colavito shared with five others dating back to 1901. Eight more have since joined the group.

The other not-to-be-forgotten game occurred April 18, 1960, the first time he wore a uniform other than one with "Indians" across his chest. It was Opening Day, and he'd been traded to the Tigers for Harvey Kuenn. Colavito was angered by the deal, as were most Tribe fans, many of whom—though fewer in number—are still angry.

As for the highlight memory, Colavito described it virtually pitch by pitch, including an "odd" question he'd been asked during batting practice that night. "I'd had only three hits in my previous 28 times at bat, and a writer asked me about my 'slump.' I told him I didn't believe in slumps, that I was never in a slump," he recalled. And then he proved it.

Colavito walked in the first inning, then his barrage of homers got underway against Jerry Walker in the third inning.

He said he hit a fastball down the left field line. "That was the only one I wasn't sure would go out. I thought it would hook foul," Colavito said.

Home runs Nos. 2 and 3 were off reliever Arnold Portocarreo in the fifth and sixth innings. "Both times I hit sliders over the left-center field fence," he said.

When he batted in the ninth against Ernie Johnson, Colavito knew he had a chance for the record. "I didn't feel any pressure," he said. "Actually I was relieved because I'd had three hits and felt I was out of the bad thing I was in," he said, careful to avoid calling it a "slump."

"I remember telling Herbie [Score], I'd be happy with a single. I didn't try to hit another home run. I never did. I just tried to hit every ball hard. God blessed me with power and if I hit a ball hard, I knew it would go out." Rocky ended that season with a league-leading 42 homers, the second consecutive season he hit more than 40.

As for the "lowlight," as Colavito called it, "I loved it in Cleveland and I wanted to play my entire career there." Gabe Paul brought him back in 1965 in a three-team trade in an attempt to placate the fans, as well as Colavito. But it was too late. Colavito was near the end of his career, and the Indians manager in 1967, Joe Adcock, was neither a fan of Colavito nor—the truth be told—a good manager.

Adcock platooned Colavito with Leon Wagner, which angered both, and both asked to be traded. So Colavito was dealt away again, this time to the Chicago White Sox on July 29, 1967. He spent the last three years of his career as a part-time player.

Colavito finished with a career batting average of .266 that included 371 homers, 1,148 RBI, and an all-star team membership three times. Colavito returned to Cleveland as a coach in 1973 and again from 1976 to 1978; he also was a part-time broadcaster of Tribe games.

But after 1965, it never was the same for the man who had been one of the favorite players to ever wear a Cleveland uniform—and who had never wanted to give it up.

Year	Tm	G	AB	R	H	HR	RBI	SB	BB	SO	BA
1955–59, 65, 66	CLE (8 yrs)	913	3185	464	851	190	574	9	468	478	.267
1960–1963	DET (4 yrs)	629	2336	377	633	139	430	6	346	301	.271
1964	KCA (1 yr)	160	588	89	161	34	102	3	83	56	.274
1967	CHW (1 yr)	60	190	20	42	3	29	1	25	10	.221
1968	LAD (1 yr)	40	113	8	23	3	11	0	15	18	.204
1968	NYY (1 yr)	39	91	13	20	5	13	0	14	17	.220
Total		1841	6503	971	1730	374	1159	19	951	880	.266

Sam McDowell

Sam McDowell's best pitch isn't the 100-mph fastball he threw in the 1960s and early 1970s when he was compared to "a young Sandy Koufax."

That's also when it was being said that the six-foot-five southpaw had a chance of becoming the greatest strikeout pitcher the game had ever known, even better than Nolan Ryan, who holds the record with 5,714.

But, obviously it never happened to McDowell, aka "Sudden Sam." And, instead of all he could have been and done—by his own admission—McDowell said, "I was the biggest, most hopeless and violent drunk . . . during my 15 years in the major leagues."

Actually, saying that McDowell "retired" is a misnomer. "I was kicked out because of my drinking," he said. Even stronger self-criticism prefaced that remark when McDowell bluntly stated, "There is absolutely no doubt in my mind that I would be in the Hall of Fame if I had not been a drunk."

Those who saw McDowell pitch—when he was sober—would agree. Unfortunately, he waited too long to do what he is doing now. A totally dried-out, sober, recovering, and reformed Sudden Sam is a certified alcohol and drug counselor. As such, he is devoted in his career to helping other present and former athletes and family members with emotional and psychological problems, and to help them avoid taking the road that got McDowell kicked out of baseball.

In addition to his work in sports, McDowell also is a certified addiction counselor at the master's level and conducts Employee Assistance Programs (EAP) upon request for nonsports-related organizations. He also serves in various capacities with the "Baseball Assistance Team" and works on special assignments with all teams in "crisis intervention" (suicide prevention) as a therapist and counselor.

Several years ago McDowell founded and developed the "City of Legends," located in Clermont, Florida. It is an ongoing project of which McDowell is chief operating officer. He is partnered with Dr. Michael Ray, a nationally known sports medicine orthopedic surgeon.

The main purpose of the City of Legends "is to assist former athletes—those who played baseball, football, basketball, hockey . . . whatever, and their families, with social, health, medical, even housing, and whatever other problems they have."

McDowell's enthusiasm is overwhelming. Gratifying, too, to those who recognized his potential for greatness as he was earning the nickname "Sudden Sam," then threw it all away. "Let me put it this way," McDowell said. "If I'd had the kind of help that I can provide players now, Nolan Ryan might not be baseball's leading strikeout pitcher."

It's interesting to go back with McDowell to the beginning of his pitching career, and the night in Cleveland in 1961 when the "Sudden" part of his nickname came into being. It's a story told often by Charlie Manuel, the former manager of the Indians who was then with the Minnesota Twins.

As Charlie told it, he was next to a couple of Twins players, Jim Lemon and Harmon Killebrew, who had struck out against McDowell in one of Sam's first appearances on the mound. Killebrew was asked what he thought about "that rookie pitcher" (McDowell), and he replied, "Wow, his ball sure gets up there all of a sudden"—and thus was born a legendary nickname.

But that part of McDowell's life is passed. Now he is involved in what he calls "bigger and better things."

But, considering his raw potential back then, it is frustrating to many, though not to McDowell himself, he says. "It isn't frustrating to me because I wouldn't be where I am now, and doing what I'm doing—and helping others from doing what happened to me."

Year	Tm	W	L	ERA	GS	CG	SHO	IP	H	R	BB	SO
1961–1971	CLE (11 yrs)	122	109	2.99	295	97	22	2109	1603	805	1072	2159
1972–1973	SFG (2 yrs)	11	10	4.36	28	4	0	204	200	109	115	157
1973–1974	NYY (2 yrs)	6	14	4.20	22	2	1	143	115	74	105	108
1975	PIT (1 yr)	2	1	2.86	1	0	0	34	30	11	20	29
Total		141	134	3.17	346	103	23	2492	1948	999	1312	2453

Herb Score

One morning in March of 1957, Hank Greenberg, general manager of the Indians, received a phone call from Joe Cronin, the general manager of the Boston Red Sox.

"We could use a top flight pitcher and we'd be interested in buying that kid [Herb] Score that you've got. A pitcher like that would be worth a million dollars . . . are you interested?" Cronin wanted to know.

Before reporting what Greenberg told Cronin it's important to establish the details of the situation in baseball at that time. In 1957 a player's salary as high as $100,000 a year was unheard of . . . the minimum salary was somewhere around $7,500 (it is now $440,000), and in 1957 the Red Sox franchise had just been sold for $4 million.

Greenberg, who'd been part of the group that paid $3.9 million to buy the Indians franchise, reportedly replied to Cronin, "You mean that you would pay us one million dollars for Score?"

Cronin said, "One million dollars in cold cash. Just say the word."

Greenberg replied, "Joe, we would not sell that kid for two million dollars. He is not for sale at any price."

That was almost 20 years before Marvin Miller came along and broke major league baseball's ironclad reserve clause, opening the door to free agency and multimillion dollar salaries.

As for that 23-year-old kid, Score, he was the American League Rookie of the Year in 1955 when his won-lost record was 16–10 with 245 strikeouts in 158 innings. He was even better in 1956 when he went 20–9 with 263 strikeouts in 246 innings.

Tris Speaker, the one-time manager of the Indians who worked in the team's front office, said, "If nothing happens to that kid, he could be the best ever."

Then came 1957. Score won two of his first three decisions and made his fifth start on May 7 against the New York Yankees at the Cleveland Municipal Stadium. The second batter of the game, Yankees infielder Gil McDougald, lined Score's second pitch back at him. "I never saw it until the ball was about two feet away," said Score. It struck him just below his right eye.

Needless to say, Score was badly injured, actually lucky to be alive. He spent the next three months in the hospital and, also fortunately, was able to still see with his right eye.

However, Score, trying to come back in the final month of the 1957 season, was never the same, though he steadfastly refused to attribute the problem to his eye injury. He insisted he'd hurt his elbow when he came back. Joe Gordon, then the Indians manager, thought it happened because Score changed his pitching motion after he was injured.

All Score knew was, "I could still throw as hard, but my pitches never had the same movement they did before I hurt my elbow."

Score had losing records the next two years (2–3 in 1958 and 9–11 in 1959) and was traded to the Chicago White Sox. But nothing changed. In the next three seasons his overall record was 6–12, and he retired.

The Indians hired him in 1964 as a broadcaster—a job he loved and the fans loved him—for 34 years through 1997, when he retired at age 64.

Then another disaster struck Score. He was involved in an automobile accident and was hospitalized again.

Ironically, it happened as he was leaving Canton, Ohio, the morning after he'd been honored at a banquet as Broadcaster of the Year.

A series of strokes followed and the outstanding pitcher and equally outstanding broadcaster—who had a legion of friends from his baseball and radio days—died in 2008 at age 75.

Year	Tm	W	L	ERA	GS	CG	SHO	IP	H	R	BB	SO
1955–1959	CLE (5 yrs)	49	34	3.17	100	41	10	714	490	288	458	742
1960–1962	CHW (3 yrs)	6	12	4.25	27	6	1	144	119	76	115	95
Total		55	46	3.36	127	47	11	858	609	364	573	837

Luis Tiant

When Luis Tiant was called up from Portland of the Class AAA Pacific Coast League on July 19, 1964, his age was listed as 24, which probably was at least six—and likely ten or more—years light.

But no matter. The always-smiling Cuban gave the Indians six good seasons before they traded him to Minnesota, and when he retired in 1982 he had to be closer to 52 than 42.

Also, when he retired, Tiant had won 229 major league games (with 172 losses) in 19 seasons. He was a 20-game winner three times, pitched three one-hitters, led the AL with a 1.60 earned run average in 1968 and was a member of the American League all-star team three times.

When the Indians promoted Tiant in 1964, it was to pitch the second game of a doubleheader in New York, with the expectation they would send him back to the minors after the game. But Tiant spoiled the plan by firing a four-hitter and striking out 11 in a 3–0 victory. He went on to produce a 10–4 record and his belated major league career was underway.

And though he was listed as a "rookie" in 1964, he was far from being inexperienced.

In December 1969 he was traded with pitcher Stan Williams to the Twins for pitchers Dean Chance and Bob Miller, third baseman Graig Nettles, and outfielder Ted Uhlaender. It proved to be a good deal for both teams.

Minnesota released Tiant—probably thinking he certainly was by then too old—and he was signed by Atlanta for only two months and was released again. Two days later Boston signed him, to the good fortune of not only Tiant but also the Red Sox.

For the next seven-plus seasons, beginning in May 1971, Tiant was a regular starter and fan favorite, especially in 1975 when the Red Sox won the pennant. Tiant went 18–14 and won 20 games on three other occasions.

When the Red Sox gave up on Tiant, also probably thinking he was too old in 1978, he went on to play for three other clubs—New York Yankees, Pittsburgh, and California—before he retired for good in 1982.

Tiant, a clubhouse prankster and good humor man, also known as "El Tiante," probably earned his determination to pitch for so many years from his dad, Luis Clemente Sr. The elder Tiant was a southpaw who also gained notoriety as an excellent pitcher for the New York Cubans and Philadelphia Eagles of the Negro League in the middle 1940s, and the Mexican League before that.

In fact, when it was announced by the Indians they were promoting Luis Jr., from Portland, he was greeted with open arms by Al Smith, a third baseman-outfielder with the Tribe. "I remember his dad [from the Negro League] and if he is half as good as his father was, we're getting a helluva pitcher," Smith was quoted then. Obviously, he was correct.

As Smith also said after Luis Jr. won his first three games for the Indians, "I can tell he learned a lot from his father because of the way he rocks and twists and turns before he releases the ball, which is the way his dad pitched."

Also interesting is the way the Indians "found" Tiant. He was pitching for the Mexico City Tigres, owned by Bobby Avila who played second base for the Indians in the 1950s. Avila recommended the Indians purchase Tiant and told them, "Never mind how old he looks, when you see his stuff you'll think he is only 21."

Avila also was correct.

Year	Tm	W	L	ERA	GS	CG	SHO	SV	IP	H	R	BB	SO
1964–1969	CLE (6 yrs)	75	64	2.84	160	63	21	12	1200	939	431	432	1041
1970	MIN (1 yr)	7	3	3.40	17	2	1	0	92	84	36	41	50
1971–1978	BOS (8 yrs)	122	81	3.36	238	113	26	3	1774	1630	709	501	1075
1979–1980	NYY (2 yrs)	21	17	4.31	55	8	1	0	332	329	173	103	188
1981	PIT (1 yr)	2	5	3.92	9	1	0	0	57	54	31	19	32
1982	CAL (1 yr)	2	2	5.76	5	0	0	0	29	39	20	8	30
Total		229	172	3.30	484	187	49	15	3486	3075	1400	1104	2416

Jim "Mudcat" Grant

The coming storm—the era of free agency and multimillion dollar contracts—was still a decade away. But even in 1964, when the average salary in baseball was $15,000 and the highest salary was less than $100,000, financial times were tight.

That was the background for the trade that initially was so devastating to Jim "Mudcat" Grant, one of the Indians' most popular players and one of their potentially best pitchers.

"I wanted to spend my entire career in Cleveland," he said. "Cleveland is where I started, where I got my first chance, and the only place I liked as much as Lacoochie," which is in central Florida where Mudcat was born and threw his first baseball.

Grant was considered one of the Tribe's best young pitchers, along with Sam McDowell, Tommy John, Gary Bell, and others in the farm system. As a rookie with the Tribe in 1958, Grant was 10–11 and in mid-June 1964 was a regular starter.

His career record was 67–63, and included 15–9 in 1961 when he was 25 years old and still developing. In those days the Indians' goal was to reach one million in annual attendance, although they were able to reach that plateau only in 1959, when it was announced at 1,497,976.

All of which often led to player trades based more on payroll and less on players' production or abilities, which was a primary factor in Mudcat's departure. It was a surprise and great disappointment to him and many Tribe fans—although it turned out to be a very good deal for him and Minnesota, if not the Indians.

So why did they give up one of their best and still-developing pitchers? When the mid-month paychecks were being signed by president Gabe Paul, he did so with his eyes on the calendar, as well as the Indians financial ledger. Back then the trading deadline was June

15, and it had become evident that the Indians were not going to contend—again—for the pennant. But the Twins were, and they needed another starting pitcher.

So Grant was traded. The Indians received journeyman third baseman George Banks and veteran pitcher Lee Stange. Banks played 17 games for the Indians into mid-1966 when he was released. Stange's record for Cleveland was 13–12, and he also was gone by mid-1966. The amount of money the Indians received for Grant was never disclosed, though it had to be substantial.

Grant proceeded to pitch the Twins to the pennant in 1965, becoming the first African American pitcher to win 20 games. His record was 21–7, and he won two more games against Los Angeles in the World Series. The *Sporting News* named him the Pitcher of the Year.

Mudcat pitched four more seasons for the Twins with an overall 50–35 record, was traded to the Dodgers, then was selected by Montreal in the expansion draft in 1969 when he became a relief specialist. Next he was dealt to St. Louis, then to Oakland, Pittsburgh, and back to Oakland in 1971, after which he retired with a 145–119 career record, 53 saves, a one-hitter against Washington in 1965, and twice being selected to the American League all-star team. Then it was back to Cleveland, the city he loved almost as much as Lacoochie.

After briefly considering a comeback attempt as a reliever for the Indians, Mudcat took a front office job, did some television broadcasting of Tribe games in the 1970s, and also got into the entertainment business with a song-and-dance group called "Mudcat and the Kittens."

And so, the bottom line on his baseball career was that, while he didn't want to leave Cleveland, all turned out well for Grant after he did.

But not for the Indians.

Year	Tm	W	L	ERA	GS	CG	SHO	IP	H	R	BB	SO
1958–1964	CLE (7 yrs)	67	63	4.09	165	50	8	1214	1090	602	565	707
1964–1967	MIN (4 yrs)	50	35	3.35	111	36	10	780	783	340	163	377
1970–1971	PIT (2 yrs)	7	4	3.41	0	0	0	87	87	35	30	26
1970–1971	OAK (2 yrs)	7	2	1.85	0	0	0	150	129	35	36	67
1969	STL (1 yr)	7	5	4.12	3	1	0	63	62	31	22	35
1968	LAD (1 yr)	6	4	2.08	4	1	0	95	77	29	19	35
1969	MON (1 yr)	1	6	4.80	10	1	0	50	64	33	14	20
Total		145	119	3.63	293	89	18	2442	2292	1105	849	1267

Andre Thornton

The plane was 37,000 feet over the Pacific Ocean, en route to Cleveland from Hawaii where major league baseball had concluded its annual winter meetings. The date was December 10, 1976, which is when the Indians made one of their strangest "announcements."

They had been mildly active participants in the trading market, although general manager Phil Seghi complained that "you guys in the media don't seem to like what we've done."

The Indians were coming off an 81–78, fourth-place finish in the six-team East Division of the American League, and it seemed to "you guys"—or us, as well as the fans—that more needed to be done.

Then halfway across the Pacific, a stewardess came down the aisle looking for the "Cleveland press corps." When she found us, she read a note she'd scribbled during a ground-to-air phone call from "a man named Phillip Seghi." It said, "Tell the reporters I made a deal after the meetings ended to get Andy Thornton, and that I'd talk to them tomorrow."

So there we were without a chance to interview Seghi for another 24 hours. We could only speculate who Seghi might have traded to get Thornton. It was Jackie Brown, a pitcher who went 9–12 for the Expos in 1977 and retired. That made it a good trade, as Thornton was the long ball–hitting first baseman the Indians needed. He also happened to be one of the classiest players in the game and played for the Indians for 10 seasons.

In those 10 seasons, Thornton smashed 214 home runs, including highs of 33 in 1978 and 1984. His statistics included 749 RBI and a .254 batting average. However, when he was acquired, another perceived problem arose: the Indians planned to use Thornton mainly as a designated hitter, although their most

consistent hitter in 1976 was Rico Carty, whose only position was as a designated hitter. "It'll work itself out," shrugged Seghi, and manager Frank Robinson agreed.

They were right. Thornton went on to play 131 games in 1977, mostly at first base, and he batted .263 with 28 homers and 70 RBI. Carty was the designated hitter in 127 games and hit .280 with 15 homers and 80 RBI.

But it was Carty's last season in Cleveland, as he went back to Toronto in 1978.

Thornton, as the Indians full-time designated hitter, became a two-time all-star in 1979, was elected to the Ohio Baseball Hall of Fame and the Greater Cleveland Sports Hall of Fame, was the Tribe's Man of the Year in 1984, and received the "Golden Tomahawk" award four times as the team's Most Valuable Player. He also received the Roberto Clemente award in 1979, given annually to a major league player who best emulates Clemente's commitment to his community.

Shortly after joining the Indians, Thornton and his family were involved in a tragic automobile accident. His wife and daughter were killed; Andre and his son, Andre Jr., survived. Thornton remarried in 1979, and he and his wife, Gail, raised sons Jonathon and Dean.

Among the many tributes paid Thornton is this oft-repeated praise by Hall of Fame pitcher Jim Palmer, which perhaps best describes the kind of player Thornton was: "Whenever I face the Indians," Palmer said, "I only worry about one thing. I don't want to face Andre Thornton in the late innings. If I do, I'll walk him. He can change a 1–0 win into a 2–1 loss with one swing of his bat."

All of which, along with all the other testimonials on behalf of Thornton, should erase any doubts that were raised in the minds of Seghi's press corps back there in 1976.

Year	Tm	G	AB	R	H	HR	RBI	SB	BB	SO	BA
1977–1987	CLE (10 yrs)	1225	4313	650	1095	214	749	39	685	683	.254
1973–1976	CHC (4 yrs)	271	795	122	212	30	122	7	163	136	.267
1976	MON (1 yr)	69	183	20	35	9	24	2	28	32	.191
Total		1565	5291	792	1342	253	895	48	876	851	.254

Albert Belle

Any (should that be every?) article about controversial Albert Belle usually (should that be always?) starts the same way: he is either loved or hated, respected or disrespected, and fans are either glad or sorry he's gone. Take your choice.

All this because his temperament and other indiscretions, prior to his injury-forced retirement, have irreparably soiled his reputation as one of the greatest hitters to play the game.

Love him or hate him: For leading the Indians to their first pennant (1995) in 41 years when he flirted with breaking Roger Maris's single-season home run record; for being the American League RBI leader with 148 in 1996; for hitting the most home runs (242) in an Indians career before it was broken by Jim Thome (with 334); and for being described as a "perfectionist" in everything he did, sometimes to a fault.

Respect him or disrespect him: For a series of incidents, including intentionally trying to injure a player (Milwaukee second baseman Fernando Vina), hitting a heckling fan with a thrown baseball, and throwing a baseball at a photographer; for using a "corked" bat for which he was suspended ten days and fined $25,000; for cursing a female television reporter for which he was fined $50,000; for being obstinate and surly with the media; for refusing on occasions to sign autographs; and, of course, for being unwilling to re-sign with the Indians upon reaching free agent status.

Glad or sorry he's gone: for retiring after 12 seasons (1989–2000).

Certainly, Albert Belle belongs among Indians legends. However, even though Belle regularly produced Hall of Fame numbers, he almost certainly will not be elected to the hallowed Hall. He has been rejected twice and no longer is eligible to be listed on the general ballot.

Belle's only chance now would be for him to be reconsidered by the Veterans Committee composed of former baseball executives, some veteran writers, and current members or players already in the Hall of Fame.

The reason he no longer is listed on the annual ballot considered by members of the Baseball Writers Association of America is because he did not receive enough votes in the second of two previous elections. The rules require that if a player fails to receive at least 5 percent of the votes cast, his name is removed.

In Belle's first time on the ballot in 2006 he received 40 votes, or 7.7 percent of the 520 votes cast. The following year he was named on only 19 votes, or 3.5 percent, of the 545 ballots, after which he was no longer eligible.

Is that recrimination by the large number of writers who felt they had been verbally abused by Belle? Very possibly, just as it seemed to Belle himself—and many others—that he should have won the AL Most Valuable Player Award in 1995 when he hit 50 homers and drove in 126 runs. Instead, he finished second to Mo Vaughn of Boston (whose statistics were not as good but whose personality was much more agreeable).

Belle played for the Indians from 1991 through 1996. The next year he signed with and played two years for the Chicago White Sox and, as a free agent again in 1999, he agreed to a multimillion-dollar contract with Baltimore, which, upon his retirement in 2001, was still required to pay him $39 million over the next three years.

Belle was forced to retire because of an arthritic right hip that could not be surgically repaired; it prevented him from even considering a comeback.

Now living in Arizona with his wife and four children, Belle spends most of his time, as he has said, "being a part-time house father and a full-time golfer"—and out of the public eye.

Year	Tm	G	AB	R	H	HR	RBI	SB	BB	SO	BA
1989–1996	CLE (8 yrs)	913	3441	592	1014	242	751	61	396	622	.295
1997–1998	CHW (2 yrs)	324	1243	203	374	79	268	10	134	189	.301
1999–2000	BAL (2 yrs)	302	1169	179	338	60	220	17	153	150	.289
Total		1539	5853	974	1726	381	1239	88	683	961	.295

Kenny Lofton

It was the first of several good acquisitions by John Hart upon his promotion to general manager when Hank Peters retired in 1991. Not only did it establish Hart as a shrewd evaluator of talent but it also made other clubs aware that the Indians no longer were going to play the game as they had for so long—that under Hart they were going to be, as he said, "proactive."

That first deal indicated also that Hart trusted his scouts' opinions and was willing, even eager, to make a move. It brought to Cleveland a basketball player from the University of Arizona named Kenny Lofton—or, better stated in this case, an *outfielder* from the University of Arizona.

Lofton had been a 17th-round choice of the Houston Astros in baseball's 1988 amateur draft. As Hart said, "Granted, we're not talking about an established star . . . we're talking about a guy who can run like hell. And as one of our scouts said, 'All this kid [Lofton] has to do is make the ball bounce twice in the infield and he's got a hit.' Besides, we weren't giving up a front liner to get him."

Lofton didn't make an immediate impact, but he came close in his first year (1991) with the Astros.

With the Tribe in 1992 he was off and running. Literally. He batted .300 four times in the next five seasons, including a high of .349 in 1994, and he stole 325 bases (in 395 attempts).

Most longtime Tribe fans who were in front of their television sets the night of October 17, 1995, will long remember a game in Seattle during the American League Championship Series. The Indians needed to win to reach the World Series and were clinging to a 1–0 lead in the eighth inning. Lofton singled, stole second, and, with two outs, scored—*all* the way from second—on a passed ball. The Indians won, 4–0, vaulting them into the World Series for the first time in 41 years.

Lofton left after the 1996 season, when the Indians were eliminated from the AL Division Series by Baltimore. Hart traded him to the Braves with pitcher Alan Embree for outfielders Marquis Grissom and David Justice.

But Lofton returned as a free agent in 1997 and played the next four seasons in Cleveland. He left again, this time unhappily in 2002, which launched a whirlwind series of moves, via trades or free agency, establishing Lofton as one of the most frequent travelers in baseball. He wore nine different major league uniforms in the next seven years.

The traveling began, according to Lofton, when Hart declined to re-sign him in 2002 (allegedly for budgetary constraints) and traded him to Atlanta.

It angered Lofton, who said then, "I've done everything they've asked me to do in Cleveland and I thought I would be rewarded. I guess they rewarded me by trading me."

But times change. So do people. Lofton admitted to having been unhappy with the Braves, and Hart admitted he was sorry for the way he "rewarded" Lofton, which he attempted to correct when he re-signed the center fielder in mid-2007. Lofton played 52 games for the Tribe that season and retired at age 40.

But it was quite a run for Lofton—and the Indians—while it lasted, never mind what happened between his good start and later.

Year	Tm	G	AB	R	H	2B	3B	HR	RBI	SB	BA
1992–96, 1998–2001, 2007	CLE (10 yrs)	1276	5045	975	1512	87	518	452	611	652	.300
1991	HOU (1 yr)	20	74	9	15	0	0	2	5	19	.203
1997	ATL (1 yr)	122	493	90	164	5	48	27	64	83	.333
2002	SFG (1 yr)	46	180	30	48	3	9	7	23	22	.267
2002	CHW (1 yr)	93	352	68	91	8	42	22	49	51	.259
2003	CHC (1 yr)	56	208	39	68	3	20	12	18	22	.327
2003	PIT (1 yr)	84	339	58	94	9	26	18	28	29	.277
2004	NYY (1 yr)	83	276	51	76	3	18	7	31	27	.275
2005	PHI (1 yr)	110	367	67	123	2	36	22	32	41	.335
2006	LAD (1 yr)	129	469	79	141	3	41	32	45	42	.301
2007	TEX (1 yr)	84	317	62	96	7	23	21	39	28	.303
Total		2103	8120	1528	2428	130	781	622	945	1016	.299

Omar Vizquel

He has been called a "magician," an "acrobat," once even a "jockey"—and best of all an "all-star shortstop" who surely was destined to one day be a "Hall of Fame shortstop."

Omar Vizquel came to the Tribe in 1994 as a defensive wizard and became so much more as the Indians went to the postseason playoffs every year from 1995 to 1999, again in 2001, and to the World Series in 1995 and 1997.

Unfortunately, the Indians let Vizquel become a free agent in 2004 because they were unwilling to pay him a large bonus. They believed that, at age 37, he would be unable to maintain his high level of performance. Obviously they were wrong.

The time Vizquel was called a "jockey" was when, as a teenager, he attended a tryout camp hoping to be offered a contract. He wasn't . . . and the scout didn't even give him a chance to show what he could do. Instead, Vizquel was told to "go to the racetrack and be a jockey."

Now, maybe six or seven inches taller, Vizquel commands the respect of teammates, opponents, and fans alike.

There's not much more anybody could ask of Omar Vizquel.

It all began for him with Seattle in 1989 as a 22-year-old defensive star, though he hit a creditable .252 in 650 games for the Mariners before he was traded to Cleveland. It turned out to be one of general manager John Hart's best acquisitions: Vizquel for shortstop Felix Fermin and outfielder Reggie Jefferson.

In Vizquel's 11 seasons (1994–2004) with the Tribe, he batted .283 in 1,478 games, including a career high .333 in 1999.

And, to the chagrin of many, he was far from finished when the Indians decided he was not worth a $4 million bonus. He went to San Francisco where he played four seasons (2005–8), then to Texas (2009), the Chicago White Sox (2010–11), and—not necessarily *finally*—to Toronto (2012–present).

Several years ago when members of the Indians 1948 World Series champion team held a reunion in Cleveland, they were asked to compare Vizquel with their shortstop (and manager) Lou Boudreau. Bob Kennedy, the right fielder on that 1948 Tribe team and a major league scout in 1998, said, "Vizquel is better than Boudreau or Marty Marion or Luis Aparicio or Ozzie Smith or any shortstop I've ever seen. He might be the best shortstop that ever played the game."

Vizquel won nine consecutive Gold Glove awards (1993–2001), and he also was a member of the all-star team each of his 11 years in Cleveland. He tied the AL record for the most consecutive errorless games by a shortstop (95) in 2001. That also was the season he proved that he was a stand-up guy who never dodged an interview the few times he had a subpar game.

A prime example occurred at the end of his errorless streak in a game in which he committed three miscues. Prior to the game, Vizquel was interviewed and talked about his nearly flawless fielding when he was playing for Seattle. "But, thankfully, I never had another game like the one I made three errors," he said. Except that he did later that very night. He made three errors, all of which contributed to the Indians losing the game.

Afterward, when many players would be hiding in the trainer's room to avoid the media Vizquel sat in front of his locker and explained how he misplayed each of the three errors.

All of which goes to show that while Omar Vizquel is small in stature, there can be no doubt that he is a "big" man in so many other ways.

Year	Tm	G	AB	R	H	HR	RBI	SB	BB	SO	BA
1994–2004	CLE (11 yrs)	1478	5708	906	1616	60	584	279	612	586	.283
1989–1993	SEA (5 yrs)	660	2111	223	531	6	131	39	173	208	.252
2005–2008	SFG (4 yrs)	542	1926	232	510	11	177	67	180	186	.265
2009	TEX (1 yr)	62	177	17	47	1	14	4	13	27	.266
2010–2011	CHW (2 yrs)	166	511	54	137	2	38	12	43	63	.268
2012	TOR (1 yr)	60	153	13	36	0	7	3	7	17	.235
Total		2968	10586	1445	2877	80	951	404	1028	1087	.272

Manny Ramirez

However strange his antics were—and they often were *very* strange—they usually were shrugged off with a "that's-Manny-being-Manny" comment. It pertains to Manny Ramirez, a very unconventional and, in the opinion of many, a plain old slovenly individual, but one who could hit a baseball better than almost everybody.

Which is what Ramirez did. He hit baseballs with ferocity, often and far, first for the Indians and then Boston, each for eight seasons, then the Los Angeles Dodgers for three, and next the Chicago White Sox in 2010 and Tampa Bay in 2011.

And then, while serving a 50-game suspension for violating Major League Baseball's drug policy, in 2012 Manny retired, ending his professional baseball career with a .312 batting average, 555 home runs, and 1,831 RBI.

It all began for the Dominican Republic–born and New York–reared Ramirez in 1991 when he was 19 and the Indians made him their first-round choice (13th overall) in the amateur draft. Two years later he made his major league debut in the final month of the 1993 season and, as the statistics would tend to indicate, he appeared overmatched, getting only nine hits in 53 at bats for a .170 average.

Except that two of the hits were home runs, the first of 236 he hammered for the Indians before he signed with Boston as a free agent in 2001 for what was then said to be the largest financial contract in sports history. Indeed, in Ramirez's strange but profitable baseball career, it has been reported that his earnings, from 1993 through 2011, totaled nearly $209 million.

Of his career in Cleveland, Ramirez's .592 slugging percentage is the best in the history of the Indians, and he was a member of the AL all-star team six times. It was during that 1999 season that the Indians batting coach Charlie Manuel said of Ramirez, "The more I see him, the more I believe Manny is the best right-handed hitter I've ever seen."

Ramirez helped the Red Sox win the pennant in 2004 and the pennant and World Series in 2007. In eight years in Boston, Ramirez batted a composite .312 with 274 homers.

Among his homers for the Indians was one that many longtime Cleveland fans will remember. It happened on July 16, 1995, as the Indians were fighting to win their first pennant in 41 years. The score was tied, 4–4, in extra innings of a televised game against Dennis Eckersley, the Athletics ace relief pitcher. Ramirez hammered an Eckersley fastball *practically out of sight,* into the left center field stands at the Oakland Coliseum. And, as the TV camera zoomed in on Eckersley, viewers could read his lips as he exclaimed, "Wow!"

Worth retelling, too, is one of the best Manny-being-Manny stories. One night before an Indians game, Ramirez needed something he had left in the glove compartment of his truck but didn't have time to go out for it himself. So he gave his keys to a clubhouse attendant and asked him to run the errand for him.

When the attendant returned to the clubhouse, his eyes were wide in wonderment because, among the items in the glove compartment of Ramirez's truck, was a paycheck in the amount of $10,000. It was more than a month old and Ramirez had never cashed the check. When the attendant gave Manny the check, Ramirez said, "Thanks . . . I forgot all about that."

Again, that was Manny being Manny.

Year	Tm	G	AB	R	H	HR	RBI	SB	BB	SO	BA
1993–2000	CLE (8 yrs)	967	3470	665	1086	236	804	28	541	780	.313
2001–2008	BOS (8 yrs)	1083	3953	743	1232	274	868	7	636	849	.312
2008–2010	LAD (3 yrs)	223	735	130	237	44	156	3	138	157	.322
2010	CHW (1 yr)	24	69	6	18	1	2	0	14	23	.261
2011	TBR (1 yr)	5	17	0	1	0	1	0	0	4	.059
Total		2302	8244	1544	2574	555	1831	38	1329	1813	.312

Charles Nagy

Charlie Nagy wasn't the kind of pitcher who blew batters away as did Sam McDowell or Bob Feller or some others in the class of those two fireballers.

But Nagy knew *how* to pitch, *how* to get batters out . . . and *how* to win. It's the reason Nagy is now a pitching coach for the Arizona Diamondbacks. He ended his Indians playing career in 2002 with a won-lost record of 129–105. Those 129 victories place Nagy among the top-ten winners in Indians history, led by Feller (266), Mel Harder (223), and Bob Lemon (207).

And though his fastball didn't match McDowell's or Feller's or some others, Nagy nonetheless is sixth in career strikeouts with 1,235 in 1,942 innings. Nagy never won 20 games, though he came close with 17 three times—in 1992, 1996, and 1999—and 16 once and 15 twice.

Something else that embellishes Nagy's credentials is that he made 192 consecutive starts—never missing even one—from October 3, 1993, until May 16, 2000. And when he finally did miss a start it was to undergo arthroscopic surgery for the removal of bone chips in his elbow. Nagy also missed most of the 1993 season when he had surgery to repair a torn labrum muscle in his shoulder.

Nagy was a first-round choice (17th overall) of the Indians in the 1988 amateur draft, after he'd pitched for the U.S. team that won a gold medal in the Olympic Games.

He was a member of the American League all-star team in 1992, 1996, and 1999 and holds a distinctive record, one that might never be broken, unless the designated hitter rule is dropped by the American League. Nagy was the first pitcher in 30 years to get a hit, which he did in the 1992 game with a single off John Smoltz in the second inning of a game with Atlanta.

When talking about Nagy's emergence as a confident and effective starter for the Indians, it's interesting to recall an incident from the early days of his professional baseball career. It happened in midseason of 1990, and Nagy was then in his second year pitching for Canton-Akron of the Class AA Eastern League.

The Indians had a doubleheader that night, and suddenly the pitcher scheduled to work the nightcap got sick. An urgent call was made to Canton to summon a pitcher—any pitcher—and Nagy turned out to be the guy because he was scheduled to pitch the following night. So Nagy made a quick trip to Cleveland and reported to the clubhouse where manager Johnny McNamara was waiting. Nagy walked in and McNamara told him to get into a uniform and out on the field as quickly as possible.

When Nagy went to the locker room to get dressed, McNamara said to Herb Score, a Tribe broadcaster, now deceased, "Herbie, quick . . . go in and slap some color in the kid's face. It looks like he's scared to death."

Maybe Nagy was. He lasted only four innings. But whether he was scared or not, Nagy learned fast how to win. Which is one of the qualities that should make him a good coach.

After leaving the Indians as a free agent in 2002, Nagy signed with the San Diego Padres but retired after pitching five games with an 0–2 record.

He returned to the Cleveland organization and served as a special assistant to the general manager, then donned a uniform again as a minor league pitching coach for the Angels, Padres, and Diamondbacks, where he is currently the pitching coach.

Primarily because he knows how to pitch—and especially how to win.

year	Tm	W	L	ERA	GS	CG	SHO	IP	H	R	BB	SO
1990–2002	CLE(13 yrs)	129	103	4.51	297	31	6	1942	2173	1054	583	1235
2003	SDP (1 yr)	0	2	4.38	0	0	0	12	15	7	3	7
Total		129	105	4.51	297	31	6	1954	2188	1061	586	1242

Jim Thome

It's not too early to make plans to attend Jim Thome's induction into the National Baseball Hall of Fame, even though it can't happen until 2018 at the earliest. The reason for the delay? Players must be retired five years before being eligible for election. And in Thome's case the only question would be when, not if.

Thome signed as a free agent to rejoin Philadelphia in 2012. Later that season he was traded to Minnesota and then to Baltimore. Because his contract extends through 2013, his waiting period would end with the 2017 season unless he retires at the end of 2012.

Actually, Thome's ticket for baseball immortality was punched on August 15, 2011, in the seventh inning of a 6–4 Indians victory at Comerica Park in Detroit off Tigers left-hander Dan Schlereth. It was Thome's second homer of the game and 600th of his career, making him the eighth player in the history of baseball to reach that plateau. He went on to hit 612 homers by the end of 2012—and 600 is the "magic" number that literally ensures election to the hallowed Hall. As if that's not enough, Thome has had 13 walk-off home runs in his career. That's a major league record, and it beats Babe Ruth's career record by one.

Accredited members of the Baseball Writers Association of America (about 500) do the voting, and to be elected a candidate must be named on at least 75 percent of the ballots. Thome, one of the most popular and highly respected players in baseball, began his journey to Cooperstown when he was 19 and selected by the Indians in the 13th round of the 1989 amateur draft. He made his major league debut with the Tribe on September 4, 1991.

He has been called a throwback to the days when players wore their uniform pants high. He doesn't "hotdog" around the bases after slugging a home run and reminds fans to say "please" and "thank you" when seeking his autograph. He also is the kind of professional athlete—of which, unfortunately, all are not—who is easy to interview and to admire, which adds to the expectation of his being elected to the Hall of Fame. "Why not?" he asks rhetorically when commended for his courtesy and professionalism. "I am doing what I always wanted to do, and I love it."

While Thome started his major league playing career in Cleveland, he left in 2003 as a free agent to rejoin his friend and longtime mentor, Charlie Manuel, to sign with the Philadelphia Phillies. In so doing, he rejected what would have been a lucrative contract to remain with the Indians—or also to go elsewhere—and strongly denied he signed with the Phillies because they offered more money.

Thome subsequently was traded to the Chicago White Sox (2005) and signed as a free agent with Minnesota (2010). He was traded to the Indians in the final month of the 2011 season, obviously to allow him to hit his 600th homer for his fans in Cleveland. As a free agent again in 2012, he rejoined his mentor and friend, Manuel, with the Phillies.

Thome's first career homer came on October 4, 1991, in Yankee Stadium off Steve Farr. His next 603 homers (through 2011) were slugged off 395 different pitchers, most of them (nine), off Rick Reed of the Twins.

Through his 42 years and more than 23 seasons, dating back to that Class AA Eastern League ballpark in Canton, Ohio, in 1989, and certainly through all the hits and RBI and 600-plus home runs, Jim Thome is still the same James Howard Thome from Peoria, Illinois, that he was in 1989.

And whenever his Hall of Fame plaque is unveiled, it certainly will be where it belongs, where baseball's all-time best players are memorialized.

Year	Tm	G	AB	R	H	HR	RBI	SB	BB	SO	BA
1991–2002, 11	CLE (13 yrs)	1399	4711	928	1353	337	937	18	1008	1400	.287
2003–5, 12	PHI (4 yrs)	391	1341	243	348	101	281	0	268	406	.260
2006–9	CHW (4 yrs)	529	1770	335	469	134	369	1	362	544	.265
2009	LAD (1yr)	17	17	0	4	0	3	0	0	7	.235
2010–11	MIN (2 yrs)	179	482	69	128	37	99	0	95	151	.266
2012	BAL (1 yr)	28	101	8	26	3	10	0	14	40	.257
Total		2543	8422	1583	2328	612	1699	19	1747	2178	.276

Sandy Alomar Jr.

When the deal was announced on December 6, 1989, it caught most Indians fans by surprise. "Why are they trading Joe Carter? He's the best player we've got. And who's this guy Alomar? Is he that old guy who played second base? Are they crazy?"

Which is how it was when John Hart pulled off another of his good trades in the process of rebuilding the Indians. Hart sent Carter to San Diego for three players: two young, relatively unknown players, catcher Sandy Alomar Jr. and infielder Carlos Baerga; and veteran outfielder Chris James.

Little did the average Tribe fan realize that the four-player trade, even at the expense of Carter, would result in the advent of what has been called the "Era of Champions" in Cleveland. That would be 1994 through 2002, during which the Indians won two pennants in 1995 and 1997 (and came within one strike of capturing the franchise's first World Series championship in 49 years), along with six division championships.

Also, little did fans realize that Alomar—not the "old guy who played second base," but his son, Sandy Jr.—would become one of the best young catchers in the game and get even better. Even more significant, Alomar would end his active career in 2007 to become a leading candidate as a major league manager.

Certainly, giving up Carter was a gamble, but one that proved to be correct. He was going on 30 years old and was coming off a season in which his average fell from .271 to .243. And though he'd hit a career high of 35 homers in 1989, in Hart's opinion, Carter's ability was descending, not ascending. Besides, as Hart evaluated the situation, he knew the Indians weren't going to win soon—or even over the long haul—unless he brought in some new, young,

eager-to-win players, such as Alomar and Baerga.

It is unfair to Baerga to give all the credit to Alomar for the Indians renaissance. But there is little doubt that Alomar was the primary motivator if, for no other reason than the way he handled the young pitchers coming up and the veteran pitchers Hart brought in. "I was very happy to come over [to Cleveland], even though I didn't know much about the organization," said Alomar. "Over there [in San Diego] I was stuck behind a veteran catcher [Benito Santiago]. I wanted a chance to play."

He got it in Cleveland and made the most of it. The then 24-year-old Alomar batted .290 with nine homers and 66 RBI in 132 games, and he won the American League Rookie of the Year award in 1990. When he retired as a player 20 years later, his career batting average was .273.

He also was a "take-charge" guy, as a catcher—and captain—should be.

Alomar's only problem were the knee injuries he sustained that shortened his career.

His 11 years with the Indians were outstanding. Alomar's cumulative batting average was .277, which included 92 homers and 453 RBI. It was a shame the Indians couldn't keep him. Alomar left as a free agent after the 2000 season and signed with the Chicago White Sox.

He went on to play for Colorado, the White Sox again, Texas, the Los Angeles Dodgers, and briefly the New York Mets before his knee problems forced him into retirement in 2007. And then, finally, it was back to Cleveland. The Indians hired Alomar as a coach in 2010 and he remained with the Tribe, despite several opportunities to go elsewhere as a coach.

All of which leaves one to wonder whether Alomar is the Tribe's—or some team's—manager-in-waiting.

Year	Tm	G	AB	R	H	HR	RBI	SB	BB	SO	BA
1990–2000	CLE (11 yrs)	985	3409	416	944	92	453	24	165	386	.277
1988–1989	SDP (2 yrs)	8	20	1	4	1	6	0	3	4	.200
2001–02, 03–04	CHW (5 yrs)	265	773	80	199	19	94	1	35	68	.257
2002	COL (1 yr)	38	116	8	31	0	12	0	4	19	.267
2005	TEX (1 yr)	46	128	11	35	0	14	0	5	12	.273
2006	LAD (1 yr)	27	62	3	20	0	9	0	0	7	.323
2007	NYM (1 yr)	8	22	1	3	0	0	0	0	3	.136
Total		1377	4530	520	1236	112	588	25	212	499	.273

Carlos Baerga

There always was something mysterious, almost irrational about the way Carlos Baerga was suddenly traded without advance notice or even speculation, to the New York Mets on July 29, 1996.

It happened in the wake of the Indians most successful season, 1995, when they won their first pennant in 41 years, during which Baerga was a major contributor. The deal—Baerga (and Alvaro Espinoza) for Jeff Kent and Jose Vizcaino—was never really explained by front office chief John Hart or manager Mike Hargrove. The closest anybody came to offering even a quasi explanation as to why Baerga was sent away was a comment attributed to an anonymous Indians official who said, "[Baerga] became the victim of his own excesses."

There was speculation that he had fallen from favor with Hargrove, though it seemed implausible based on a subsequent remark by Hargrove. "The day we traded Carlos . . . was maybe the toughest day I've had as a manager," Hargrove said. "He was the heart and soul of our club . . . when you mention the Cleveland Indians, the first thing [fans] thought of was Carlos Baerga." Then, he added, "Carlos just lost his way a little bit." But otherwise, there never was a solid reason given for trading Baerga.

Actually, when the Tribe acquired Baerga (with catcher Sandy Alomar and outfielder Chris James) in a deal that sent Joe Carter to San Diego, many fans were displeased. That was prior to the 1990 season, and the acquisition of Baerga and Alomar was the forerunner of what would become the "Era of Champions" in Cleveland.

It lasted eight years, through 2001, produced six first-place finishes in seven American League Central Division seasons, included two pennants (1995 and 1997) and two World Series appearances—and 455 consecutive sold-out games at Jacobs Field.

As Hargrove pointed out, it was Baerga (along with Alomar) who was a key figure in jump-starting the Indians revival on the field and at the gate. Between 1992 and 1995 Baerga was a member of the all-star team three times. He had over 200 hits in two of those years. On April 8, 1993, Baerga set a major league record by hitting two home runs from each side of the plate—both in the same inning, the seventh, against New York. Two months later he hit three home runs in one game against Detroit.

But in 1996, leading up to the inexplicable trade that sent him to the Mets, Baerga had only 113 hits in 424 at bats with ten homers in 100 games. The change of scenery didn't help, and for the remainder of 1996 his average fell to .193. It improved—to .281 and .266 the next two years—though his power remained virtually dormant, and he was released by the Mets.

Baerga tried to make a comeback in 1999 with the Padres in 33 games and Indians in 22 but was unsuccessful. He didn't play in 2000 and 2001, but he tried again in 2002 with Boston, 2003 and 2004 with Arizona, and 2005 with Washington, but to no avail.

On September 30, 2005, Baerga played his final game. Little note was made as to how well he did, or even that he played.

His baseball career was finished at age 36—and all the questions that had been asked and were left unanswered, remained unanswered.

And so, whatever it was that happened to Carlos Baerga, a major figure in one of the Indians' best trades, is still a mystery.

But nevertheless, based on how it all began for Baerga—and lasted until "he lost his way"—the chubby, strong-armed, switch-hitter with surprising power was indeed a Tribe "legend," if only too briefly.

Year	Tm	G	AB	R	H	HR	RBI	SB	BB	SO	BA
1990–96, 99	CLE (8 yrs)	941	3666	549	1097	104	565	49	198	386	.299
1996–1998	NYM (3 yrs)	306	1061	104	283	18	116	2	49	111	.267
1999	SDP (1 yr)	33	80	6	20	2	5	1	6	14	.250
2002	BOS (1 yr)	73	182	17	52	2	19	6	7	20	.286
2003–2004	ARI (2 yrs)	184	292	37	91	6	50	1	24	32	.312
2005	WSN (1 yr)	93	158	18	40	2	19	0	7	17	.253
Total		1630	5439	731	1583	134	774	59	291	580	.291

David "Buddy" Bell

He was a fan favorite from the beginning. The son of a major league player, he was Hollywood handsome with blond hair and blue eyes, good minor league statistics, and always (OK, *usually*) a smile.

When he arrived in Cleveland as a rookie, they changed his position from third base to the outfield, a move he accepted without complaint. This was Buddy Bell, who did many things with grace, even accepting an unpopular trade to the Rangers seven years later, though it was a deal that displeased him as much as it did Tribe fans.

But Bell went to Texas again without complaint and continued what might have been a Hall of Fame career had it not ended on his own volition. When he quit playing in 1988, Bell had 2,514 hits and a 20-year career batting average of .279

After his playing career with the Indians, Rangers, Cincinnati, and Houston between 1972 and 1988, Bell managed three teams (Detroit, Colorado, and Kansas City) for nine years.

He served as the director of minor league instruction for the Chicago White Sox (1991–93), rejoined the Tribe as a minor league coach in 1994 and 1995, managed the Tigers from 1996 to 1998, returned to Cincinnati as the Reds minor league coordinator in 1999, managed the Rockies from 2000 to 2002, returned to the Indians as a consultant in 2002 and their bench coach in 2003 (under Eric Wedge), worked for the Chicago White Sox in 2004 as their director of player development, managed the Royals from 2005 to 2007, and then returned to a front office job with the White Sox as their director of player development.

Bell, whose father Gus was an outfielder for Pittsburgh, Cincinnati, New York Mets, and Milwaukee from 1950 through 1964, was a 16th-round selection by the Indians in the 1969 amateur draft.

Unfortunately, Buddy Bell's debut in professional baseball was sidetracked early when he suffered an injury to his right knee in a benefit basketball game. It required immediate surgery, and Bell underwent six more knee operations in subsequent seasons.

He also played most of his career with epilepsy. His is a story that should provide inspiration to others so afflicted. Bell admitted he was terrified when he was first diagnosed with the disease, "But as soon as my family and I heard that most cases were controllable by medication, we all pulled together," said Bell. "I worried whether I could still play, but once I got used to [the medication], pretty soon I was back on my game."

Bell was elected the Indians Man of the Year in 1973 when he led the American League third basemen in putouts and double plays, and he went on to win six Gold Glove awards and five all-star rings.

His best season was 1980 when he batted .329 with Texas, which obviously gave rise to regrets that the Indians traded him two years earlier for Toby Harrah.

When he joined the Indians as a 20-year-old rookie in 1972, Bell was coming off an outstanding season as Wichita's third baseman in the Class AAA American Association where his manager had been Ken Aspromonte. When Aspromonte was hired to manage the Indians to replace Alvin Dark the following season, he insisted that Bell be given a chance to play in the major leagues, even though, at the time, the Tribe's third baseman was Graig Nettles. Consequently, Bell played the outfield the entire season. When the season ended, Nettles was traded, and Bell returned to his natural position.

And finally, it's obvious that the Bell's bloodlines are baseball oriented as all three of Buddy's sons were selected in baseball's amateur drafts—David (who played for three major league teams from 1995 to 2006) Michael, and Ricky.

Year	Tm	G	AB	R	H	HR	RBI	SB	BB	SO	BA
1972–1978	CLE (7 yrs)	987	3712	462	1016	64	386	24	297	332	.274
1979–85, 1989	TEX (8 yrs)	958	3623	471	1060	87	499	24	335	297	.293
1985–1988	CIN (4 yrs)	386	1391	194	370	43	184	6	185	118	.266
1988	HOU (1 yr)	74	269	24	68	7	37	1	19	29	.253
Total		2405	8995	1151	2514	201	1106	55	836	776	.279